Hilda Gott

1920 - 2012

Life on Her Watch

Philip Wadner

2021

Published by Cade Books

©2021 Philip Wadner

All rights reserved.

ISBN 978-0-9931987-9-3

Philip Wadner has asserted his right under the Copyright, Designs and Patents Act 1988 to be identified as the author of this work.

This book is sold subject to the condition that it shall not, by way of trade or otherwise, be lent, resold, hired out, or otherwise circulated without the publisher's prior consent in any form of binding or cover other than that in which it is published and without a similar condition, including this condition, being imposed on the subsequent purchaser.

For Gary, Jeff, and Laura.

Acknowledgements

I am especially indebted to Christine Wadner and Hilary Worker for inside information about their mother, Barbara Jones with help from Helen Roe, David Gott and Wendy Mann for details about James Allan Gott, Frank Pyrah for his photographs of old haunts, Gavin Scott Brooker for the photograph of Alpine Vale Cottage, Pamela and David Hoole for finding details of the Buick, Moira Kilkenny at the Warkworth Historical Society, and friend and author Dr. John Craddock for reading and commenting on my drafts. Finally, this family memoir would not have been possible without the extensive background material available on the internet, and I express my gratitude to all those anonymous contributors who have made family history research possible in ways it has never been before.

Preface

This is my third family history book. After researching my paternal grandfather's life and that of my maternal grandmother, neither of whom I had much knowledge of, I took on the challenge of writing about my mother-in-law Hilda Brooker née Gott, someone who I knew even less about.

Like most people born before the Second World War, Hilda was not one to talk about her life. Even though I was frequently in her company between when I married her eldest daughter in 1970 and when she died in 2012, she said little that disclosed her past.

Early discussions about Hilda's life often ended with a casual observation that she didn't *do* anything worth writing about. Indeed, she had a quiet, unimposing personality with a reputation for reliability and common sense.

Not only does this memoir record that she did, indeed, do a great deal worth writing about but also that on her watch the people around her lived a life filled with accomplishments they would otherwise not have achieved.

Although my limited knowledge of Hilda's life provided a starting point for this book, Hilda's two daughters and her niblings were able to give me leads without which I would have floundered. Using the resources of the internet, they turned up a plethora of ideas to explore further. That is how family history research works; the more the researcher discovers the more questions are raised.

The natural conclusion of the previous statement is that a family history can never be completed and that there will always be more to discover and loose ends to tie up. That is the case here. But if one of Hilda's successors wants to know more and carries out further research into their ancestry, this memoir will have accomplished more than I could have hoped for.

Phil Wadner
Summer 2021

Contents

Acknowledgements iv

Preface v

Introduction ix

Ancestry 1

    The Gotts 1

    The Larges 3

    Florence Large and James William Gott 5

Victor Geoffery Brooker (1919 - 1993) 9

Hilda Gott 17

    Benson Street, Middlesbrough (1920 - 1942) 17

    Military Service (1942-1946) 26

    Home to Benson Street for Three Months (1946) 33

    Samlesbury Hall Lodge (1946 - 1948) 38

    Warkworth (1948 - 1950) 45

    Longbenton, Newcastle (1950 - 1951) 48

    Ravenside (1951 - 1955) 50

    Styford (1955 - 1956) 59

    Greenside (1956 - 1960) 67

    Kempston (1960 - 1963) 74

    Cotswold Close (1963 - 1971) 86

    Gloucester Road (1971 - 1973) 97

    Pax Hill (1973 - 2010) 102

Marston Moretaine (2010 - 2012) 121
Siblings Florrie, Alice and Allan 125
    Florence Emily Gott (1909 - 1977) 125
    Lily Gott (1913-1913) 131
    Alice Gott (1915 - 1980) 132
    James Allan Gott (1922 - 2016) 137

Introduction

There are many ways to present a memoir. I have chosen to remain accurate to chronology as far as possible to smooth the flow between Hilda's life events.

Hilda's parents were James William Gott and Florence Large, and that is where her story begins. Almost. Before embarking on her parents' potted history, there is an outline of Hilda's paternal and maternal ancestry tracing her forebears back to around the 16th century.

Victor Brooker, Hilda's husband, is introduced after her parents. Although this might appear contextually incorrect, his life ran parallel to Hilda's before they met. Keeping their early years separate provides clarity for each narrative, until fate brought them together at the end of the Second World War.

Victor was not one to remain in one place for long, and the couple frequently moved home until their later years when they eventually settled down. The book makes use of these changes of address to signpost Hilda's life and provide a logical progression to her story.

Some sections are more detailed than others because they all rely on fading memories from long ago. Some are dim recollections to which I have added my own interpretation guided by research, and others are more comprehensive and add colour to Hilda's life.

Memory is selective by human nature, which implies some intentionality behind what is remembered and what is not. With writing a memoir comes a responsibility to the subject. That means balancing the good with the bad, the highs with the lows, and happiness with sorrow. Furthermore, some details have been deliberately omitted to guard against opening old wounds.

For completeness, the book concludes with a short vignette of the lives of Hilda's siblings. They played a huge role in her early years, and she in theirs. Although contact with them waned towards the end, mostly because of the physical distance between them, Hilda stayed in touch as best she could.

Ancestry

The Gotts

Records of Hilda's paternal ancestors can be found as far back as Thomas Gott, born in Halifax, West Yorkshire, in 1510. Henry VIII had just been crowned and was married to Catherine of Aragon. When Thomas was four years old, invading Scots led by James IV battled with the English at Flodden Edge in Northumberland and were defeated, with the Scottish King and some 10,000 of his army killed. By the time Thomas Gott was in his twenties, the printing press had been invented, England's monasteries were closed down and the Anglican bible was published.

Thomas' son, also Thomas Gott, was born in 1530, and his son, yet another Thomas, was born in Kildwick, Yorkshire in 1555 and baptised on 20th October that year. He married Anne Iles from Keighley in 1575 and they had three children, Grace, William and Thomasina.

There has to be some uncertainty surrounding the interpretation and linking of records from over 500 years ago, but from the 1600s there can be more confidence in their accuracy.

Thomas and Anne's only son William married 17 year old Margaret Blakey from Kildwick on 4th March 1605. They had 14 children, the last one born in 1629 sadly dying shortly after birth.

William and Margaret's son John Gott was born in Kildwick on 3rd June 1626. He married local girl Florence Harper in 1649 and they lived just over a mile away at Steeton on the main road to Keighley. John was a self-employed weaver. Working the land in the West Riding of Yorkshire became less popular in the 17th century, and farmers began to combine agriculture with mining, metal-working, weaving and tanning. Over the following centuries, the area would become a major centre for the textile industry. John and Florence had thirteen children between 1650 and 1669. Their eighth child, Isaac, was born in 1658.

Isaac married Anne Illingworth from Bingley, and set up home there shortly after the wedding. Anne gave birth to a son, Isaac after his father, in 1681. Isaac Jr. wed Mary Beetham from Bingley in 1704. They had a daughter Anne in 1706, and a son, another Isaac, in 1710. It would be five more years before Mary gave birth to Thomas, but tragically he died at the age of two. A year later, on 20th April 1718, Mary died giving birth to their fourth child who Isaac named Thomas after the son they had lost.

At the age of 37, fifteen months after Mary died, Isaac married again, this time to Magdalen Clark from Belchford, Lincoln. Magdelene was 17 years his junior and delivered Isaac five more children between 1721 and 1730. Magdalen died in Bingley on 21st April 1746, and Isaac outlived both his wives reaching 71 years of age by the time of his death on 27th June 1752.

It was Isaac and Mary's last child Thomas Gott who provided the next link down Hilda's family tree. He married Elizabeth Bewley in Beverley, York and they had a son, also Thomas, in 1735. On 10th January 1771 at the age of 36 he married Elizabeth Simpson from Crambe. They had three daughters and one son between 1772 and 1780, and naturally the son was named Thomas. At the age of 29, in 1803 he married Emma Brown and they settled in Gilling, a small village about three miles north of Richmond. Although one of their children was named Thomas, the spell was broken and it was their fourth child Joseph, born in 1816, who would become Hilda's great grandfather.

Joseph married Margaret Spofforth Huddlestone from Malton, Yorkshire, on 20th July 1844 when they were both aged 21. They were to have 13 children over the following 22 years, 12 of whom would be Hilda's great aunts and uncles on her paternal line. George Gott, Joseph and Margaret's seventh child and Hilda's paternal grandfather, was born 25th August 1855 in Low Hutton, Ryedale, North Yorkshire.

George married Emma Charlotte Stebbings from Norton-on-Derwent on 1st August 1876 and, like George's parents, he and Charlotte were to have many children: four daughters and four sons (Hilda's paternal uncles and aunts). Hilda's father James William Gott was their fifth child and was born in Keighley on 6th November 1885.

The Larges

Hilda's maternal family line can be traced back to the time of Shakespeare's England in the 1600s. Queen Elizabeth I died in 1603 and in 1605 Guy Fawkes attempted to blow up the English parliament, Sir Walter Raleigh was executed in 1618, 1642 saw the outbreak of the English Civil War between the Roundheads and Cavaliers, and in 1665 bubonic plague wiped out a fifth of London's population. As though Londoners had not suffered enough, the Great Fire of London raged in 1666 destroying most of the civic buildings, old St. Paul's Cathedral, 87 churches and 13,000 houses.

Although prior to 1600 Hilda's ancestors hailed from Hampshire, by the mid 17th century they had moved south across The Solent to the Isle of Wight perhaps to escape to a more peaceful life. Edward Butcher, Hilda's 7th great-grandfather, was born in Shalfleet on the Isle of Wight in 1660.

Shalfleet is a small village in the north west quarter of the island about three miles east of Yarmouth and a mile inland. Shalfleet means shallow stream, and is named after the Caul Bourne which passes through the village. Early records show the population in 1800 to have been around 500, and even today only about 1500 people live in Shalfleet.

Edward Butcher and his descendants will almost certainly have worked the land, growing mostly wheat and oats and to a lesser extent barley, peas, potatoes and turnips. As well as excellent arable land, there was plenty of first-rate pasture for rearing livestock.

In 1706, Edward's son, also Edward, married Elizabeth Dore from Freshwater, situated on the coast at the western end of the island and famous for its rock formations. Elizabeth's ancestry can be traced back to the mid-1500s. Her grandfather John Dore was born in Freshwater, although her grandmother Margaret Vinson was from Gatcombe in Hampshire.

Two generations down through Thomas Butcher born to Edward and Elizabeth in 1709, and Thomas' son William Butcher born 1745, both in Shalfleet, William married Mary Smart from Bedfordshire in 1768. William and Mary moved to the mainland making their home in Framlingham, Suffolk. William and Mary's son, also William, was born 1771 in Framlingham.

William met Sarah Temper, who lived not far away in his village of Framlingham, in 1791 when he was 20 years of age. Sarah was 15 when she became pregnant, and gave birth to a son John just after she turned 16 later that year. William and Sarah lived together in his parent's house for four years. They married in 1795 and set up home in Mildenhall not far from the Cambridgeshire border.

William and Sarah's son John Butcher married Susan Burgess, also from Mildenhall. They had five children starting with Robert in 1811 through to Martha in 1827. All were born in their parents' home town.

At the age of 18, Martha married James Large, a young agricultural labourer from the small village of Redgrave near Diss. They were to bear two sons and three daughters all born in Mildenhall. James' youngest brother William Butcher married Caroline Bell from Littleport in 1840 and they made their home in Downham. Their second son, John Large, was Hilda's grandfather.

Aged 13, John Large was working as an agricultural labourer in Mildenhall and when he reached the age of 21 he married William and Caroline's daughter, his first cousin, 19 year old Matilda Butcher from Prickwillow in Cambridgeshire, on 31st October 1879. Their first child Sarah was born in Prickwillow in 1880, but shortly afterwards the couple moved to the north-east of England and the following five sons and three daughters (Hilda's maternal uncles and aunts) were born in Grangetown, an area on the eastern edge of Middlesbrough, Yorkshire.

John and Matilda's third child and Hilda's mother, Florence Large, was born in 1884.

Florence Large and James William Gott

Iron ore was discovered near the small farming village of Eston around 1850, and the sharp influx of many hundreds of people from all across Britain to work in the ironstone mines helped the area to grow from a couple of cottages into a thriving mining town. By the time Florence was born, the underground caverns made to extract the ironstone stretched some three miles, almost to Guisbrough.

The ironstone mines led directly to the birth of the iron and steel industries along the River Tees and the building of Middlesbrough, which grew from a small farming hamlet with a population of 25 in 1801. Florence's father John Large had left behind the rural county of Suffolk and his employment as an agricultural worker around 1882 to become a steelworks labourer. Almost every man in the locality was employed in either the mining or steelworks industry, confirmed by a quick glance at the census records for 1881. Next door to John and Matilda lived an ironstone miner, then next an engine driver in ironstone mines, and two doors down in the other direction another ironstone miner and yet more of the same for the following four houses.

Although the rapid growth of the industry made many people rich, the same could not be said for the miners and steelworkers. The mines were dangerous, and the miners were paid piece work determined by the number of tubs they filled. Injuries were frequent, leading to time off with no pay with disastrous results for the family. The steelworks were equally dangerous. Having spent a 12 hour shift sweating in a hot, smoky and noisy environment a steelworker would return home exhausted. In the late 19th century, the blast furnaces, cranes, stacks of heavy steel, airborne toxins and the ever-present risk of explosion meant that serious injury, ill-health and fatalities were the norm.

Florence grew up in Eston at 51 Woods Street on the eastern edge of Middlesbrough. Life was hard for her and her siblings. Their mother would have looked after running the household budget on a meagre income, and be responsible for clothing and feeding the family. Florence left school at 14 to contribute to the family income, although by then her father and 18 year old brother John were both working as blast furnace labourers so the family were not living on the breadline.

In 1908, 24 year old Florence married James William Gott. When James had left school, he had become a brickyard labourer the same as his father and two older brothers William and George. William was attracted to the north east by the prospect of a better job in the steel industry and moved to Binks Street in Linthorpe around 1905 taking employment as a blast furnace labourer. Binks Street cuts the corner between Linthorpe Road and Cumberland Road, and is little more than 100 yards from Benson Street. The original houses are gone, and the area is now mostly given over to a car park and the Linthorpe Community Centre.

James' parents followed William's example, and also upped sticks to Middlesbrough. The family moved to 7 Benson Street, Linthorpe. Unlike his father and brother George, who worked in the cement and brick industry, James took a job as a park gardener with Middlesbrough Council.

After their wedding at the end of 1908, James and Florence moved into 3 Benson Street, a couple of houses down from James' parents. They were to have five children. Florence Emily in 1909, Lily in 1913, Alice 1915, Hilda 1920 and Allan in 1922.

The family's home at Benson Street was a two bedroom terraced property with two rooms downstairs and a small kitchen stretching into the back yard. Although modern day improvements will have added a bathroom either upstairs or down, the Gotts would not have enjoyed that luxury. There was no electricity or gas, lighting would have been from oil lamps or candles and an open fire would have provided scant heating.

The front door opened into a narrow hallway with a door to the front room on the left with the stairs, again to the left, before a door at the end of the hall led into the back room. The back room had a small window looking out to a brick shed in the back yard, and a door leading to the kitchen which gave access to the yard. The stairs ran up the middle of the house to a small landing which gave access to the front and back bedrooms. None of the rooms were large. The front room was about 11 feet square, the back room 14 x 10 feet, and the kitchen 10 x 6 feet. When the whole family was living in the house, James and Florence had the smaller bedroom measuring about 11 x 10 feet, and their three daughters Florrie, Alice and Hilda slept in the front bedroom which was slightly bigger at about 11 x 14 feet. Their son Allan slept wherever he could, usually on the sofa downstairs.

3 Benson Street (centre house, present day)

James and Florence would live at 3 Benson Street for the rest of their lives. They died within a month of each other in 1947, James aged 61 and Florence 63.

Victor Geoffery Brooker (1919 - 1993)

Victor Brooker, who would later become Hilda's husband, was born on 3rd August 1919 at 4 Emmanuel Road in Cambridge almost nine months to the day after Germany signed the peace agreement that signalled the end of the Great War on 11th November 1918. Coincidentally, Armistice Day would also mark his death 74 years later.

Victor's father, Cuthbert Howard Brooker, was the fourth child of John William Brooker, a schoolmaster, and Ann Elizabeth Brooker (nee Scott). Cuthbert was born on 21st October 1880 in Withington, a leafy suburb of Manchester not far from Stockport. By 1891, Cuthbert was living with his two sisters, Evelyn and Winifred, and brother George, all older than he, as well as three younger brothers, John, Arthur and Percival, in Moss Side, a small village within the Manchester parish with a population of about 6000.

In 1901, at the age of twenty, Cuthbert, by then a member of the printing trade, married Clara Alice Booth, a cotton weaver. Clara was the same age as Cuthbert and was from Kearsley, a township about 7 miles northwest of Manchester. She was probably a weaver at the textile mill in nearby Stoneclough. The marriage certificate shows Cuthbert's father had taken up the profession of clergyman, and indeed his address at the time of the marriage is given as Prestolee Vicarage. Since there was only one church in the village, Holy Trinity, it can safely be assumed that the vicarage was close by.

Prestolee is a small village surrounded almost completely by water. It is effectively an island, with the River Irwell to the north, west and south, and the Manchester Bolton & Bury Canal to the northeast, a stone's throw from Kearsley. Almost a century later, the church was used by TV show Coronation Street as a venue for many weddings and known to fans as All Saints Church, Weatherfield.

Cuthbert and Clara were married at Bolton's Register Office on the twenty seventh of July, 1901 and their first child, Donald Eric, was born less than five months later on the twelfth of December the same year.

Donald was the first of five children, the others being Edna Margaret (1904), John (1906), Stanley (1908) and the last, Dorothy Louise who was born in 1909 by which time the family were living in Hull.

Clara Brooker died from heart failure in Fleetwood, Lancashire, in 1965 at the age of 84. The death was recorded by her first son, Donald Eric, who stated Clara to be the widow of Cuthbert Howard.

For his part in the Great War, Cuthbert joined the Royal Army Service Corps as a Private in 1915 and served in France, returning to England as a 2nd Lieutenant having been transferred to the 3rd Royal Welsh Fusiliers and commissioned in November 1917. Although his army card shows his address as Spark Bridge, Greenodd, Ulverston it also records an address, scored through, of 4 Emmanuel Road, Cambridge.

Upon his return to England, Cuthbert, who by then was thirty seven years old, married Lily Agnes Scales. Lily was nineteen, her father a verger living at 4, Emmanuel Road in the centre of Cambridge.

4 Emmanuel Road, Cambridge (centre)

The sizeable house, next door but one to a small ecclesiastical building, is now occupied by The Samaritans. On the marriage certificate, Cuthbert records his father as deceased, his marital status as widower (even though Clara was alive), and gives his address at the time of marriage as 8 South Dudley Street, London, an area in Kensington now renowned for its multi-million pound properties. Cuthbert and Lily were married on 31st March 1919 at the Church of St. Andrew's the Great, around the corner from Emmanuel Road.

Victor was born just over four months later on 3rd August 1919 at the house in Emmanuel Road. Not long afterwards, Cuthbert and Lily moved to Alpine Vale, Egton-cum-Newland, near Ulverston in the Lake District where Victor's sister, Yvonne, was born on 29th September 1921.

Alpine Vale Cottage, © Gavin Scott Brooker

Tragedy struck the family when Victor had turned four years old, when on 10th August 1923, at the age of twenty six, Lily drowned in the waters of Newland Beck, on the boundary between Egton-cum-Newland and Mansriggs. The death certificate records the findings of the inquest held the following day; Lily drowned herself whilst temporarily insane.

A week later, one Hannah Mary Hopley, 23 years of age, gave birth to a son, Dennis, at 2 Stott Lane, Salford which is now the site of the Salford Royal Hospital. Hannah, who was a hotel clerk in the Pendleton area of Salford, moved into Alpine Cottage with Cuthbert, Victor and Yvonne. Dennis' birth certificate doesn't record the name of his father, and Hannah registered his birth with her maiden name, Hopley. Victor and Yvonne's grandparents, Walter and Elizabeth Scales, were not happy with the living arrangements and tried to have the children moved into an orphanage, but Hannah resisted. Victor was not to discover the identity of his real mother until much later in life.

Shortly after Lily died, Cuthbert moved his new wife and children to Chorlton-upon-Medlock. The house was at 54 Cecil Street, within the inner city area of Manchester. Cecil Street is not far from Manchester University, but the entire neighbourhood has been redeveloped. It was there that Victor's half brother Douglas was born on 11th November 1924. Although there is no record of a marriage between Cuthbert and Hannah, Douglas' birth certificate records his mother's name as 'Brooker, formerly Hopley'.

Victor spent his childhood and teenage years around the Manchester area. His father and Hannah were to have another four children: Corryn (1927), Alan (1930), Hazel (1933), and Raymond (1937) who was born when the family rented The Old Vicarage in Mellor.

The Old Vicarage, Mellor

By the time Victor reached the age of 18, including Hannah's children before she met Cuthbert he was to have twelve siblings: one sister, four half-sisters and seven half-brothers.

Although his education had been interrupted by many house moves over the years, Victor had an above-average grasp of the English language and a profound appreciation of classical music. After leaving school, he followed in his father's footsteps and worked in the printing trade mostly at small firms producing local newspapers, limited circulation specialist magazines, brochures and bespoke stationery.

Victor enlisted in the Regular Army four months before the outbreak of the Second World War. He enlisted at Stockport and joined the Cheshire Regiment on 15th May 1939, signing up for seven years with the Colours and five years in the Reserve.

Initial training took place at Macclesfield Barracks where the first six weeks were spent learning about ranks, saluting, history of the regiment, kit inspection, rifle drill and square bashing.

After nearly three years with the Cheshire Regiment and postings in the United Kingdom, Victor transferred to the Royal Northumberland Fusiliers and embarked for the Middle East on 14th February 1942. Another transfer, this time to the Rifle Brigade while serving overseas, made up his total time spent in North Africa with the 8th Army to 18 months, earning him the Africa Star.

When he qualified as an army driver on 12th January 1941, Victor probably imagined he would be driving lorries filled with troops between war zones. He would have had no idea that a couple of years later he would be chauffeuring high ranking officers around cities in North Africa using luxurious staff cars. More often than not, expensive vehicles were chosen because they were readily available at the time. The fastback Buick Roadmaster convertible was introduced in 1936, although the one with Victor standing next to it shown in the photograph below was a later version built around 1939.

Victor Brooker (left) in North Africa 1943

Victor returned to England as a lance corporal on 2nd August 1943, the day before his twenty-fourth birthday. Declared medically unfit for further overseas service, two months later he transferred back to the Cheshire Regiment. In March 1944 he was posted to the Royal Army Service Corps at Aldershot to train as a clerk. By then he had completed five year's service and earned his war service chevrons, at the same time being awarded a Good Conduct Badge. On 31st May 1945 he passed the examination needed to be re-mustered as Clerk Group C Class II.

The war was over, but Victor still had a year to serve during which he worked as a clerk with the RASC. He was responsible for running the clerical side of the Northumberland & Durham sub-district branch at Fenham Barracks in Newcastle upon Tyne.

Victor was discharged from the army on 8th May 1946 after his seven years was completed, and transferred to the Regular Army Reserve. By this time, his father and step mother were renting Samlesbury Hall Lodge, near Preston. Victor moved back in with the family, and doubtless disclosed that while at Fenham Barracks he had met the woman who would change his life.

On 19th September 1946, Victor was discharged from the Regular Army Reserve on medical grounds. A few weeks later he received a letter from them that he had been overpaid the amount of nine shillings, and was asked to remit that amount to clear his debt. Seven years and 128 days in the army and they chased him for nine shillings!

Victor Brooker 21st July 1945

Hilda Gott

Benson Street, Middlesbrough (1920 - 1942)

Hilda was born at 3 Benson Street on 13th August 1920 following the ravages of the Great War, five years after her sister Alice.

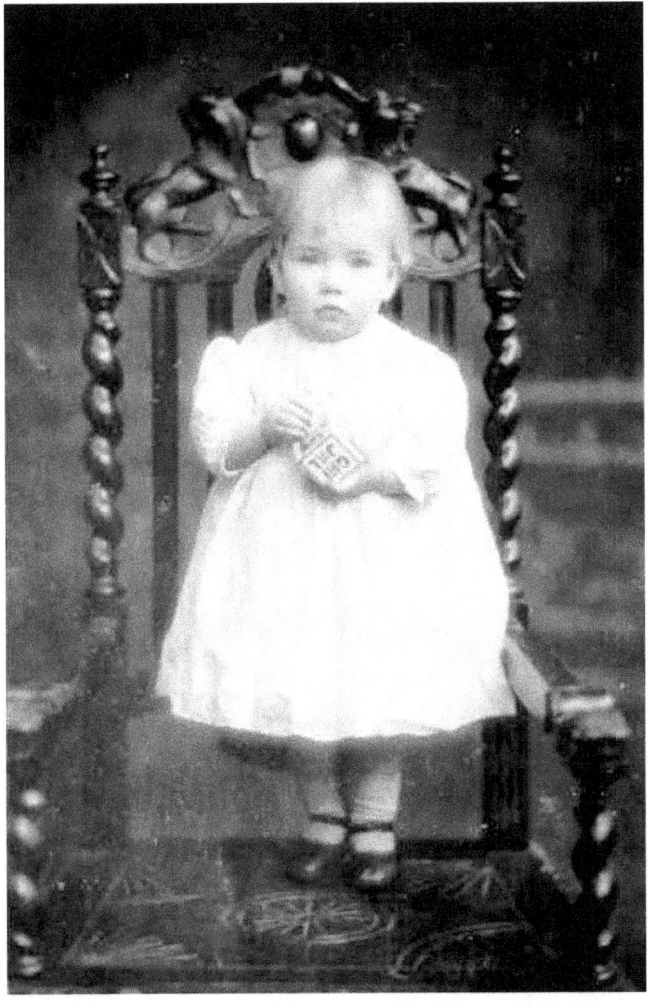

Hilda on her first birthday

The year Hilda was born was the beginning of the Roaring Twenties, and for many that signalled a decade of prosperity, fun, dance and new fashion. It also brought about a perceived decline in moral standards, as liberalism spread and the desire for freedom and equality initiated a struggle between those wishing to uphold the values and traditions of the Victorian period and others throwing restraint to the wind.

In the north east of England, however, there was little roaring going on; no short dresses, rolled down stockings, jazz clubs or carefree living. The 1920s brought a prolonged period of mass unemployment as the textile and coal industries declined and laid off workers, although for those who managed to keep their jobs living standards rose significantly. Hilda's father James had a good job working as a gardener for Middlesbrough Council, and the Gott family were comparatively comfortable.

Ever since the 1870 Education Act, most children started school when they reached five years of age and Hilda was no exception. She attended Linthorpe School, which was about a five minute walk from Benson Street. Her sister Florrie was sixteen at the time and had completed her education, but Alice was only ten and probably still attending Linthorpe School.

Original Linthorpe School ©2011 Middlesbrough Council

Built in 1871, Linthorpe School was originally known as the Wesley Day School. Split into two main buildings, it was located about a five minute walk to the south west of Benson Street on Roman Road. Only one of the original Victorian neo-Gothic style buildings still exists, the other having been replaced by a new and much larger wing in 1912 to take account of the ever-increasing population at the time.

While at Linthorpe School, Hilda won two certificates of merit from the Yorkshire Band of Hope Union, a Victorian temperance society which included a children's section. Formed in Leeds in 1847, speakers toured schools giving lectures on food and drink. One of the certificates is dated 19th November 1929, and the style of the second appears more recent so might have been awarded a year or two later.

Hilda was still at Linthorpe Senior during the Middlesbrough Centenary celebrations in 1931, and was presented with a certificate to mark the occasion.

Middlesbrough Centenary certificate 1931

From a small farm on the riverside, Middlesbrough grew into a town and coal port through the late 1820s. Between 1828 and 1833 the town's population grew as the coal shipping business took root, railway links were opened, ship-building began and major industries moved into the area. The following years saw the railways expanded to coastal areas which became popular holiday locations, and the iron and steel industry exploded.

After the summer term of 1931, Hilda moved on from Linthorpe Senior School to Hugh Bell Girls' Central. Hugh Bell's was a fee-paying school set up for educating middle class children, although unusually it was still under the control of the Board for Education. Hilda's parents would not have been able to afford fees for education, but she won a scholarship to the school and was to make a very good impression.

The school was an imposing building constructed in 1892 and named after successful businessman and Middlesbrough mayor Hugh Bell. For decades it was one of Middlesbrough's most prominent landmarks, standing proudly in the block bordered by Grange Road, Albert Road, Dunning Street and Borough Road.

Hugh Bell School c1899

The school would about a mile's walk for Hilda. She would turn left out of Benson Street, follow Linthorpe Road past St. Barnabas' Church on her left, a hundred yards on would be the main entrance to Albert Park to her right and the cemetery to her left. After another half a mile she would pass the Grand Opera House on the corner of Southfield Road, and probably turned right down King Edward's Road to cut the next corner which would take her directly to the school.

On rainy days there is a good chance Hilda would have caught a tram. These ran from Linthorpe village to the Transporter Bridge along Linthorpe Road and turned right at Grange Road, where she would get off at the corner with Albert Road. The photograph above shows that corner, with the tramlines just visible in the foreground. The trams stopped running in 1934, and were replaced by double decked buses.

Not only was Hugh Bell's building architecture striking and probably somewhat intimidating to the children attending, discipline at the school maintained authoritarian Victorian values. The staff were strict and imposed a tough regime on the pupils, who were expected to attain the highest standard of behaviour and academic achievement.

Hilda had no problem living up to expectations and was regularly placed top of her form. Her Christmas 1934 school report shows her taking first place in History, Geography, Science, Music, Needlework and Shorthand with full marks for attendance, punctuality and conduct. Although she was marked fairly high for Algebra, Geometry and slightly less so in English and Arithmetic she was poor at French coming 28th in her class of 39. Despite her excellent performance in most subjects, the best her Form Mistress could come up with was a 'Most satisfactory' which probably underlines the extremely high standards expected. The report is signed by the head mistress E.M Holmes, and also Hilda's father, James.

Over the years at Hugh Bell, Hilda won dozens of book prizes for her academic achievements. These included a copy of *The Secret Garden* for coming first in her form in 1933, Burnett's *Little Lord Fauntleroy* for exceptional progress in 1934, Locke's *The Beloved Vagabond* in 1935 for Needlework, and for Music in 1936 a copy of

Hadden's *The Operas of Wagner*. All the books were signed by the headmistress E.M. Holmes.

Hilda (left front) with school friends at Hugh Bell 1936

Hilda sat her School Certificate examinations at the end of the summer 1936 term and passed all her subjects, with credit being awarded in History and Commercial Studies.

Sadly, nothing remains of Hugh Bell School today. By the 1950s, the gradual introduction of new teaching methods showed up the inadequacies of the Victorian building. Architecturally grand though it was, Hugh Bell's was demolished in 1969 to make way for Teesside Law Courts.

To ensure that her school certificates were carefully preserved, Hilda wrapped them in a page from an October 1936 edition of the Sunday Pictorial inside which they survive to this day.

Holidays were always a special time, and many happy days were spent in the North Riding around Sleights, Egton, Whitby, Hovingham and Glaisdale. Glaisdale was the family's favourite, and they would catch a train from Middlesbrough and make the scenic journey, which lasted almost exactly one hour, under steam power. Now known as the Esk Valley line, the trains linked Middlesbrough with all their much-loved haunts.

At Glaisdale, they always rented the same cottage on the edge of the moors owned by Mr. and Mrs. Long. The Longs had four daughters younger than the Gott children, but nevertheless joined in some of the activities and became firm friends as they grew older.

Hilda and family members at Glaisdale

Allan and Hilda at Egton; Gott family at Hovingham; at Glaisdale Cottage

As well as taking her academic learning seriously, Hilda attended church and Sunday School regularly as a child. When she was ten, she kept a memento of the service at Linthorpe Parish Church, St. Barnabas, on Easter Day 1930 in the form of a card tucked inside a copy of *Little Cross Bearers* published in 1881. Hilda was confirmed by the Archbishop of York on 11th March 1935 at that same church and was presented with a small book of prayer to mark the occasion.

After Hilda left school in the summer of 1936, she worked at the Emporium located at the junction of Linthorpe Road with Grange Road. She was very good with numbers and took Commercial Studies in her final year at Hugh Bell, so began a career as a ledger clerk in the food department. Her sister Alice worked in the same building in the Mantles section, selling coats and other garments.

The beginning of the Second World War brought danger to the area, and in May 1940 Middlesbrough, with its iron and steel industries, was the first major British town to be targeted by the Luftwaffe. Many of Teesside's bridges, industrial, munitions and chemical plants, and gasworks were singled out for attack. Middlesbrough railway station was heavily bombed on 3rd August, 1942. In all, 88 civilians were killed in Middlesbrough, and over the whole of Teesside around 1,000 people were killed and more than 200 buildings destroyed.

There was a communal air raid shelter in the basement of the Emporium, so sometimes Hilda would have been working in the store by day and sheltering with her family in the basement by night. Luckily no bombs fell on Benson Street, but by the end of the war many buildings around the town were no longer standing.

Hilda continued to work at the Emporium until November 1942, when at the age of 22 she would be called upon to join the war effort.

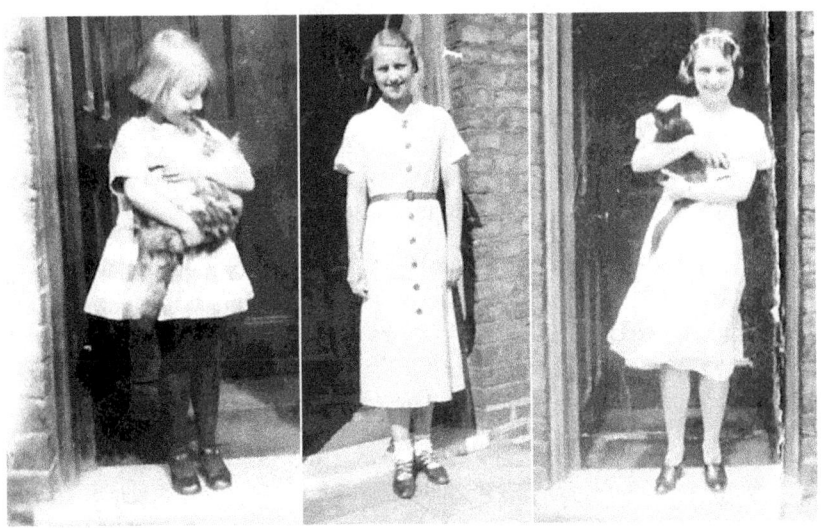

Hilda through the years at front door of 3 Benson Street

Military Service (1942-1946)

At the beginning of the Second World War the government imposed conscription for men aged between 18 and 41, but it was not until December 1941 that the scope was widened to include unmarried women between the ages of 20 and 30.

By the summer of 1943 the rules had changed again, and almost 90 percent of single women and 80 percent of married women were involved in war work. Many were employed in factories doing jobs previously carried out by men which would release them for fighting on the front line, and over 640,000 had joined the armed forces. Perhaps the most famous of all was our future Queen, Princess Elizabeth, who served in the Auxiliary Territorial Service (ATS), the women's branch of the British Army, as a driver and mechanic.

After more than 22 years living at 3 Benson Street, Hilda's call up papers dropped through the letterbox. She was instructed to join the ATS and to report to No. 4 ATS training camp at Milton Bridge in Midlothian, over the Scottish border just south of Edinburgh, on Friday 27th November 1942. Hilda signed up for the duration of the war.

Following a week of vaccinations, uniform fittings, lectures, marching, discipline training and medical and fitness tests Hilda, known then as Pte Gott. H. W/239340, sat a series of intelligence and aptitude tests. She was also required to sign the Official Secrets Act. The result of the tests, together with checks on hearing, listening and distinguishing between different sounds, would decide her fate for the remainder of the war.

Although women were not permitted to serve in battle, their duties included radar operators, anti-aircraft gun crews, and the military police as well as cooks, clerks, drivers, telephonists and orderlies.

Hilda was selected to join the Royal Corps of Signals and attend Signal School, but still had another three weeks of induction training to go through. More drills, PT, lectures, gas chamber training, and kit inspections. She was granted 48 hours leave over the weekend of 19th and 20th December, and travelled home to Middlesbrough.

ATS Signals poster from WW2

After a final drill and a formal passing out parade on 22nd December 1942, Hilda set off for the ATS Signal School at Strathpeffer in Ross-shire late evening, travelling overnight. The following day was spent settling in with her room-mate and sleeping off the train journey of the night before. Christmas Eve brought with it yet another medical inspection, an interview and more tests. Christmas Day was free time, with a festive dinner laid on and a party in the evening. Boxing Day was just a normal training day, with Hilda's first lesson on wireless heralding what would occupy her time for the remainder of the war.

The importance of the aptitude tests taken at the training camp became clear when Hilda started lessons in Morse code and how to operate radio equipment. She was also trained in the basics of electricity and how the radios worked, so she could repair the sets should they go wrong. Towards the end of the training period, there was more hands-on activity, operating radio sets using headphones and tuning into different frequencies. She would have listened in to live transmissions and practiced writing down the Morse code.

In April 1943, Hilda was posted to her first location at Newton Hall in Newton-on-the-Moor near Morpeth, and not far from Alnwick in Northumberland. Newton Hall is a large country house built in 1772, and is now a listed building.

Newton Hall (present day)

There would have been dozens of signals operators, each with their radio sets tuned to different frequencies listening in to broadcasts from the enemy, working in eight hour shifts. They would interpret the signals received in Morse code and write down the letters on gridded pads. One skill they had to learn at the training camp was to listen carefully to the sender's 'handwriting', as each sender would have their own way of using the Morse key, and report if a different operator was transmitting on their frequency.

Each listening shift lasted a gruelling eight hours, with three shifts to cover every minute through day and night. Apart from a one hour break, the signals operators would be sat at their wireless set, attached to it by headphones, listening to Morse code and writing down the messages for the whole shift. The signals would often be faint, or fade away, or have crackles and hisses which made listening difficult. It must have been exhausting having to concentrate for that long.

The coded messages were written down exactly as they were received, on a special form with three blocks of five coded letters on each line. Once a form was full, it was put aside and another started. A 'runner' would literally run with the message forms from the signal operators to a separate area which housed rows of teleprinters, each with a fast touch typist. These typists had to be specially trained, since the teleprinters had a different keyboard layout to a standard typewriter. The officer in charge would hand out the forms to the typists who would input the coded messages to their teleprinter as quickly as possible.

The signals operators had no idea who they were listening to, or what the coded messages meant, nor did they know that the messages were being sent on to Bletchley Park. There they were scrutinised by specialists and decrypted to add to the intelligence being gathered about the enemy's intentions and positions.

After three months at Newton Hall, Hilda was posted to 6-16 Woodbine Avenue, Gosforth on 7th June 1943. Situated in an affluent area of Newcastle, the large houses in Woodbine Avenue had ample space to accommodate shift teams of radio operators, and cellars where the receiving equipment could be installed away from prying eyes and ears.

6-16 Woodbine Avenue, Gosforth (present day)

Hilda worked in Gosforth for eighteen months, but her listening duties were interrupted on 23rd March 1944 when she was sent for a gas chamber test. Although chemical weapons were not generally used in combat during WWII, all members of the British Army were required to experience the conditions 'just in case'. The test involved entering a closed room containing a noxious gas with a gas mask in place, and after a while being instructed to remove the mask and breathe in the fumes. The point of the exercise was to gain confidence in the gas mask, in case it came to having to wear it during a chemical attack. Hilda passed the gas chamber test.

Hilda (front right) with ATS friends

At the end of 1944, Hilda was posted to what would be her final significant location at Thornecroft in Warkworth, where she stayed for just over a year. Apart from the war memorials which record those who lost their lives during the two world wars, and the anti-tank blocks on the beach, there is little in Warkworth to suggest it was an important outpost for listening in to enemy broadcasts.

Leaving Warkworth in January 1946, Hilda had some short postings around Northumberland taking in Morpeth and finally Fenham Barracks in Newcastle. She did not know at the time, but the posting to Fenham Barracks was going to have a profound effect on the rest of her life.

Fenham Barracks Sergeants' Mess (present day)

Hilda did not have any ambitions to become an officer and spent most of her army career as a private, although she was promoted to lance corporal towards the end of the war. She never, not ever, spoke about her work in ATS Signals.

Hilda was very popular and enjoyed many a close relationship over her time in the ATS. Sadly, the war took its toll and it was not until she was finishing her period with the army in the first few months of 1946 at Fenham Barracks in Newcastle, that she met someone destined to change her life. Also stationed at the same barracks was Victor Brooker, who was working out his army service with the RASC as a clerk at the same time Hilda was there.

Hilda was careful to include Victor's address in her address book, and as she headed for the Military Disposal Unit in York on 9th April 1946 for demobilisation, she had rather more than a casual relationship on her mind.

Lance Corporal Hilda Gott 1946

Home to Benson Street for Three Months (1946)

Victor turned out to be far more than a name in Hilda's address book, and Fenham Barracks became host to a growing attachment which ended in a proposal of marriage.

The Benson Street house must have seemed strangely quiet when Hilda returned. Her sisters Florrie and Alice were married and living elsewhere in the town, and brother Allan was serving out his time in the Royal Navy.

Victor continued to live in Samlesbury with his parents, but made the 120 mile trip to Middlesbrough as often as he could. The couple decided on an early wedding, and arranged for it to be held at St. Barnabas Church just around the corner from Benson Street on the longest day of the year, 22nd June.

St Barnabas Church, Linthorpe, Middlesbrough

Hilda's parents had just turned into their sixties, and although her father James seemed to be in fairly good health, her mother Florence had been suffering from vague stomach pain for some time and had a lump which she refused to have investigated. That did not dampen their enthusiasm for the wedding, and arrangements were soon under way.

Although Florrie would have been happy to make Hilda a wedding dress, the impact of wartime austerity was still being felt and material was very expensive and difficult to get hold of. Alice's sister-in-law Peggy had married in 1941, and managed to arrange a wedding dress. She was only too pleased to lend it to Hilda for her big day, so with a little alteration carried out by Florrie that was the perfect solution.

Hilda and Victor were married at St. Barnabas church in Linthorpe on 22nd June 1946. Witnesses to the wedding were Hilda's brother Allan and Victor's step-sister Corryn.

Wedding Group: including Allan (2nd from left), Victor, Hilda, Corryn (far right)

Hilda, 22nd June 1946

After the wedding, Hilda and Victor left for a honeymoon in Langwathby, near Penrith, in Cumbria's beautiful Eden Valley. They took the train to Darlington and from there another on what is still a spectacular route across the Pennines to Penrith, just a short hop from Langwathby. Even these days, the trip requires three changes and takes over five hours, so the newly married couple had plenty of time to wind down before arriving at their destination.

In the 1940s, Langwathby was a sleepy village on the River Eden, with a population of around 400. It has not changed a great deal, and the large green at the centre of the village is still surrounded by quaint cottages and farmhouses. Standing on the green is the Shepherd's Inn, the only place to stay, and it was almost certainly there that Hilda and Victor spent their honeymoon.

The Shepherd's Inn

Just before leaving Langwathby, the couple took a bus into Penrith and spent a day looking around the historic market town. While they were there, Victor bought Hilda a copy of Jerome K. Jerome's *The Idle Thoughts of an Idle Fellow*, a collection of witty essays, and inscribed it, 'Penrith June 28th 1946 on honeymoon'. Hilda and Victor returned to the Shepherd's Inn to spend their last night away before getting back to the start of their married life.

Although there was room for them to stay at Benson Street, it was too far from Victor's job to be manageable. He would have had to live away for the whole week, and Hilda would have been left by herself. They could not afford to rent a place of their own, so there was no alternative but to move in with Victor's father Cuthbert and his step mother Hannah at Samlesbury Hall Lodge.

There was a brief return to Middlesbrough for Hilda to pack up her belongings, and no doubt a few tears shed by her parents, then off to Samlesbury.

Victor's interest in the printing industry was fuelled by his father, who was in the trade for many years. He resumed his occupation as a printer after leaving the army and joined the Typographical Association at the Preston Branch on 30th September 1946 while working for Mather Bros., a small printing firm at 31 Lune Street, Preston. The firm opened for business in 1858 and was a well-established feature in Lune Street for over a century. The print works survived until the area was demolished to pave the way for a new access junction to Ringway.

Mather Bros. print works (tall building), Preston

In 1947, Victor moved jobs, taking a short hop to R. Seed & Sons, just along Lune Street at number 12 to work as a compositor.

Samlesbury Hall Lodge (1946 - 1948)

The original Samlesbury Hall was burnt down by Robert the Bruce in a raid on Lancashire in 1322 after he reached Preston and crossed the River Ribble. It was rebuilt a few years later, and the new hall has stood for almost 700 years. In 1924, after lying empty for 15 years, the hall was purchased by a building firm who planned to knock it down and build a housing estate. A plea for public subscription went out, and sufficient funds were raised to purchase the hall in 1925 and place it in the hands of the Samlesbury Hall Trust.

The gate lodge, which Cuthbert rented from the Samlesbury Hall Trust, was not rebuilt until around the end of the 19th century, but its architecture was designed in the same 14th century style as the main hall.

Samlesbury Hall Lodge

After he left the army, where he had already been deemed unfit for overseas military service, Victor had transferred to the Regular Army Reserve. Three months after the wedding he received notification that he had been judged medically unfit for any further military service and was discharged completely on 19th September 1946.

Shortly after the couple had moved into the lodge, Victor's step brother Douglas turned up for a family visit. He was a keen motorcyclist, and before he left that evening decided to take a ride around the grounds of Samlesbury Hall. He roared off on his motor cycle into the distance as it turned dusk, and ten minutes later the family heard him returning. His motor cycle engine was screaming louder and louder, and Hannah opened the lodge door to see what was going on. Raymond roared up the garden path and rode straight though the door and into the kitchen, his eyes like saucers and face as white as flour.

When he calmed down, Raymond explained that he was riding past the part of the hall which in medieval times had been a separate chapel, when he saw a woman dressed in a long white gown appear through the solid stone wall.

Raymond must have seen 'The White Lady', one of Samlesbury Hall's resident ghosts. The story goes that Lady Dorothy Southworth, born around 1525, was a strict Catholic. She fell in love with a young Protestant man, but their families would not accept the relationship. The couple made plans to elope, but Lady Dorothy's brother discovered the plot, murdered her lover with his sword, and secretly buried his body. Lady Dorothy was despatched to a foreign convent where it is said she died of a broken heart, but her spectre returned to the hall to wait for her lover to return.

Hilda and Victor's first child, Christine, was born at the lodge on 8th April. Although there was plenty of room, Cuthbert and Hannah decided to let the young family have the lodge to themselves. They moved to Rhoscolyn on Anglesey where they would live until December 1949 before returning to the Stockport area of Greater Manchester. Cuthbert agreed to continue paying the rent, and it was not until Hilda and Victor moved out that a misunderstanding came to light.

Hilda, Victor and Christine at Samlesbury

Christine was baptised at Samlesbury Parish Church on Sunday 25th May 1947 by the vicar, T.B. Heaton. Hilda's sister Florence, brother James Allan and his wife-to-be Marion Longhorn travelled the 120 mile journey across from Middlesbrough to sponsor her as Godparents.

The Church of St. Leonard the Less at Samlesbury is situated close to the River Ribble as it winds close by the eastern edge of Preston. It dates from the 12th century, although was substantially rebuilt in 1558 and the tower was added in 1899. The church is constructed from yellow and red sandstone (the red sandstone was used for the original building), and stone slate roof. The building was to suffer the wrath of the Scots in 1322. On his way from Preston to Samlesbury Hall, Robert

Bruce attacked the church but was unable to gain entry after a huge oak beam, which can still be seen today behind the main door, was used to bar the entrance.

Church of St. Leonard the Less, Samlesbury

Money was tight for the young couple, and Hilda's mother sent useful household items such as blankets, and a tablecloth she made from a worn sheet. She also sent overalls which Florrie no longer needed, and in July she bought a high chair so that Christine could sit at the dining table. The snag with the chair was that the place she bought it from wouldn't deliver, so she wrote to say Victor would have to collect it from Middlesbrough, over 100 miles from Samlesbury. It isn't clear where Christine was sleeping as a baby, but it would be the end of August before Victor bought a child's cot from H. Mears (Furnishers) Ltd in Preston, which was on clearance at £1.15s.

Hilda's parents, James William and Florence Gott, at Samlesbury 1947

The letters from Hilda's mother also offered useful advice on how to look after Christine. One suggested giving her some semolina and lardy pudding, well cooked, with a little custard as 'with her energy she might want a bit of solid food.' However, this was in July 1947 and Christine was only three months old, so the pudding might not have gone down too well.

Shortly after she wrote what was to be her last letter to Hilda, on 6th August 1947 Florence died. The lump she had developed which she worried was cancer and refused to seek help for, turned out to be a hernia which after a while became strangulated, and it was from that which she died. Tragically, Hilda's father James died of a massive heart attack less than six weeks later on 16th September 1947. Florrie and Bob had taken him for a break at their favourite place in Glaisdale, and he collapsed and died walking across the moors. The family agreed that he probably died of a broken heart.

Victor's only blood sibling, Yvonne, had been suffering from mental illness since she was a teenager. Yvonne was two years younger than Victor, and only one year old when their mother Lily was discovered drowned in Newland Beck at the age of 22.

In July 1947, Hannah, Victor's step mother, wrote from Rhoscolyn that Yvonne was causing trouble in the family by saying things that were causing her father distress. She suggested that Victor should take over responsibility for his sister, and arrange for a doctor to admit her to Whittingham Asylum. Hannah took Yvonne to the lodge by train, and left her there for the summer. By September 1947 she had been admitted to Whittingham, where she received electric shock treatment which it was hoped would cure her delusions if that is what they were.

Yvonne wrote on 1st November to say that she was going to be discharged from the asylum, but Hannah would not have her back in their house, fearing that she would repeat accusations she had made against her father. The superintendant at Whittingham followed up Yvonne's letter on 4th November advising that she was far from well mentally and unfit to earn her own living, He agreed that if Hannah or Victor should call for her, the asylum would hand her over, but suggested that really she should be certified and made to stay.

Victor picked Yvonne up from Whittingham on 8th November, and took her back to the lodge. She had very few clothes with her, but by the end of the month, Hannah had sent the rest from Rhoscolyn.

Looking after Yvonne proved a trying time for Victor and Hilda. She was unable to take a job, so spent all her time in the lodge. Victor was at work all day, and Hilda only got a break when she went out for groceries and essential shopping. By the spring of 1948 it became clear that Yvonne was going to have to move out, and although Hannah agreed to take her back there was a major fire at the house in Rhoscolyn and the family there lost all of their possessions. She asked Victor if he would keep Yvonne until September while they got back on their feet, but Victor had already decided that the only way out of the situation was for the young family to move into rooms where there would be no possibility of taking Yvonne. There was no other course of action but for Yvonne to return to Whittingham.

Victor and Hilda were desperate to get right away from Victor's family. Victor had been working at Seeds print works in Preston since early 1947, travelling each day on his motorcycle from Samlesbury. Seeds gave him a glowing reference on 9th June 1947 after he had been with the company only three months, but it would be only now that he used it. He applied for work as a compositor on the Northumberland Gazette at The Gazette Printing Works in Alnwick, nearly 200 miles from Samlesbury. They found rooms to rent in Warkworth, which would mean a daily journey of only about seven miles each way.

The rental agreement for Samlesbury Hall Lodge remained in Cuthbert's name after he and Hannah moved out, and there had been an unspoken understanding that Cuthbert would continue footing the rent bill of 17/6d per week. When Victor gave notice that they intended to leave, he discovered that nothing had been paid after 15th November 1947. By 5th June 1948 there was a total of £25.7s.6d owing in arrears, and the Samlesbury Hall Trust wanted the overdue amount.

Victor paid £5 towards the arrears on 5th June, and asked the Trust if they would accept £10 in full settlement for the remainder. This was agreed and, after clearing the rent account, Victor and Hilda left Samlesbury for Warkworth in Northumberland in July 1948. They left no forwarding address.

Warkworth (1948 - 1950)

Warkworth would have been very familiar to Hilda, since it was only a couple of years before when she had left her posting in the village with the ATS. She would have noticed a difference, though, between being billeted there in the war and living in rooms with Victor and one year old Christine. The family moved into Elmire House on 9th June 1948. The landlady was Mrs. Black.

Elmire House, Warkworth

Elmire House at 4 Castle Terrace near the centre of the village is an elegant building constructed of stone in 1886. Directly across the road stands the ruins of Warkworth Castle which dates back to the 12th century. The castle's heritage is uncertain, but it was mentioned in a charter of Henry II's around 1160. Over the centuries, the castle was re-modelled, added to and strengthened but was never defended in battle.

From the outside, Elmire House looks striking with its double frontage, but there were only three rooms and a small bathroom on the first floor. It is unlikely that Mrs. Black would have allowed Hilda and

Victor the run of the whole house, so they were probably restricted to the rooms upstairs. There was only very basic furniture included in the rental agreement, so on 24th June 1948 Victor went to North Lancashire Auction Mart run by E.J. Reed & Sons, 47 Fishergate, Preston and purchased two armchairs and cushions, a brass bedstead, chest of drawers, wardrobe, dining table and four chairs, a kitchen table and various other smaller items.

While completing the formalities of her late father's estate when living at Samlesbury Lodge, Hilda discovered that her sister Florrie had loaned their parents nearly £500 for the purchase of a house, although the purchase was never made. Hilda, Alice and Allan agreed that Florrie should be refunded from the estate and Hilda sent her written consent on 22nd January 1948. The remainder of the estate, about £715, was split equally between the siblings, and the distribution account was settled on 12th July 1948 shortly after leaving Samlesbury and moving into Elmire House.

Common along many of the beaches on the Northumberland coast, sea coal can be found in good measure. It is not clear whether the coal is truly washed up from the sea, or whether it is the result of coastal erosion exposing outcrops of coal seams. Warkworth beach in the late 1940s was no exception, and even today it is possible to take a walk and pick up enough coal to keep an open fire going for perhaps a day or two.

Although nothing like as bad as the winter of 1946/47, the end of February 1948 brought a flood of icy temperatures on a cold easterly wind. The south east saw over a foot of snow and drifts approaching six feet deep, but there was less in the north east although temperatures dropped to around -18°C. Hilda would go out most mornings, with toddler Christine if the weather permitted, and collect coal from the beach to keep a fire burning.

Collecting coal from Warkworth beach

After fifteen months at Elmire House Christine was two and a half years old and space was becoming cramped. In October 1949, the family moved out to a wooden cabin in New Town on the north eastern edge of Warkworth. Called 'Windale', the cabin was a summer retreat for holidaymakers left empty over the winter months.

On 3rd January 1949, Victor had been head hunted by Andrew Reid Printers in Newcastle. They invited him to attend an interview, but nothing came of their approach. However, Victor had been working at the Gazette Printing Works in Alnwick for a year and a half and was looking for a new position. He answered an advertisement placed by letterpress printers J W Hindson & Sons Ltd, Pandon House, Newcastle, in the Typographical Association Circular. Hindson's invited Victor for interview on 19th December and he landed a new job as a compositor, with a weekly wage of £12.2s 6d.

There were two problems. Warkworth was about 30 miles from Newcastle and that was a long way to travel each day, and the arrangement to rent the cabin would come to an end at the start of the 1950 holiday season probably around Easter.

It was time to move on.

Longbenton, Newcastle (1950 - 1951)

Victor started with Hindson's in February 1950, and the couple urgently needed to locate somewhere to live. Luckily, Hindson's came to the rescue and put Victor in touch with James Wilson who owned a modern bungalow about two miles north east of Newcastle's city centre at 15 Glebe Avenue in the district of Longbenton. It was probably the quietest dwelling in the street, tucked away on land at the end of a cul-de-sac of around 25 houses.

15 Glebe Avenue, Longbenton, Newcastle

The bungalow was a good size, with plenty of room for Hilda, Victor and Christine without them treading on the Wilson's toes all the time. James Wilson was a ticket and show card writer by profession and worked mostly from home. He would draw and paint the advertising slogans and images which appear in shop windows, so his business did not need much space to operate. It was probably the show cards which were the link to Hindsons, since large stores would sometimes need more than one copy of a card and Hindsons would have been able to produce them in small quantities.

Although the accommodation was very comfortable with modern facilities, the rent was £2.5s.0d each week. That equates to around £80 today, and took a large chunk of Victor's wage. Longbenton was within easy travelling distance of Hindsons, and life was easy staying with the Wilsons, but it was decided that it was time to look for somewhere less expensive to live.

After one year almost to the day, the family packed their belongings and on 24th February 1951 set off for Ravenside. The rent for their new home was set at 12s 6d each week, around a quarter what they paid at Longbenton.

Ravenside (1951 - 1955)

Ravenside Farm stands alone, and is located about three miles south east of Styford and one and a half miles west of Chopwell at Hedley on the Hill. Most of the buildings that existed in the 1950s have been knocked down and replaced by modern ones.

Ravenside Cottage, Styford

Ravenside Cottage was an extension to the end of the farmhouse. The larger building comprised the main living accommodation, with a smaller extension for the kitchen. The top and lower right images above show the buildings from the rear, and bottom left from the front although it is largely hidden from view.

Not long after moving into the cottage, the family had a visit from the Wilsons who owned 15 Glebe Avenue where they had been staying in Longbenton, Newcastle. The photograph below shows them enjoying the garden at Ravenside Cottage, but sadly Mrs. Wilson would not visit again as she died a few months afterwards.

James and Margaret Wilson visiting Ravenside

Unlike their comfortable home in Longbenton, Ravenside Cottage had no electricity or gas. On 3rd April 1951, a couple of months after moving in, Victor arrived home with a portable battery powered wireless bought from Payne & Hornsby Ltd in Gallowgate, Newcastle. It was an Ever Ready Model T Receiver and cost a massive £16.4s.9d, equivalent to about six months' rent on the cottage. The wireless had a wooden case, Bakelite knobs, and measured about 18x11x10 inches. It used valves, received long wave and medium wave broadcasts, and required a 1.5 volt battery which was quite small and inexpensive, and a 90 volt battery which wasn't.

Ever Ready Model T radio

Even though there was no power in the cottage, there was an open hearth with an oven next to it. Hilda took pride in her ability to bake, and there was no shortage of cakes and pies and hot oven-cooked meals.

1952 was the year that Christine started school. The nearest was at Chopwell (famous for the filming of the well-known Hovis advertisement), and even that was a two mile walk across fields and meadows and along the side of Milkwellburn Wood. Milkwell Burn was a stream that drained Ravenside Farm's land and ran alongside the wood to Blackhall Mill where it joined the River Derwent. The final part of the walk was along the last stretch of the railway track between Chopwell and High Spen, where it joined the main line connecting Consett and Newcastle. Built in 1896, the railway line carried coal from Chopwell Colliery, and in its heyday was transporting about 20,000 tons of coal each week.

    The new school year began in September 1952, and it would be a day that Hilda, and Christine too, would remember. Hilda had arrived at Chopwell East Infants School with Christine in good time, and the headmistress made a point of meeting her inside the main entrance to the school building with a warm welcome and a friendly chat. Hilda turned to walk away, the headmistress took Christine's hand, and all hell broke loose. Christine screamed her loudest and a tug of war took place, the school bell being knocked off its table in the process. All the teachers came out of their classrooms to see what the commotion was about.

Chopwell School c1905

As the weeks passed, taking Christine to school became less fraught, although the distance that had to be walked there and back each day was quite a trek. Some days, especially if the weather was bad, Christine would share a taxi with a young boy from a neighbouring farm not far away along the lane leading to the main Chopwell road.

Hilda was out walking with the family one day in the autumn of 1953 when she fainted, a worrying time for everyone. It was nothing serious though, and she quickly recovered. A few days later, Hilda discovered the reason behind what had happened; she was expecting a second child due to be born the following June.

Victor's father Cuthbert and step-mother Hannah returned from Anglesey in 1949 to live at Heaton Chapel, an area in the northern part of Stockport in Greater Manchester. There had been a major fire at the guest house they ran at Rhoscolyn on the island, and the owner decided to put it up for sale. Shortly after moving to Heaton Chapel, Cuthbert had a brain seizure which meant he was unable to work and the family fell on hard times. In October 1953, Cuthbert wrote to Victor saying that things were very tough between him and Hannah and asking whether he could move into Ravenside Cottage. Things did not go smoothly, and one evening he and Victor had a serious falling out. Cuthbert was told to leave without delay, and the family never spoke to him again.

Both Hilda and Victor were lovers of books, and with Christine at school and Hilary 'on the way' they invested in a set of encyclopaedias. *The Book of Knowledge* was liberally illustrated and aimed at curious young minds, although it was advertised at the time 'for all ages'. Comprising eight heavy volumes, and costing eighteen guineas, the set is still intact over sixty years later.

The Book of Knowledge

Early in 1954 Christine fell ill with severe abdominal pains, and Victor called the doctor on his way to work. The doctor diagnosed peritonitis and she was rushed to Hexham General Hospital by ambulance where the surgeons found she had a ruptured appendix. Hexham General was a new hospital initially built to treat soldiers during the Second World

War. It opened in 1940, and joined the NHS as a general hospital in 1948.

When Christine returned home after a three week stay in hospital it was without her appendix, but she had contracted whooping cough. Within a few days she passed it on to Hilda, who was reaching the end of her second trimester. During a particularly violent coughing fit in the kitchen, Hilda cracked a rib and was in great pain. Ravenside was not the best place to be in advanced pregnancy with a cracked rib and a seven year old to look after, so Hilda and Christine went to stay with sister Alice at 42 Eastbourne Road, Middlesbrough.

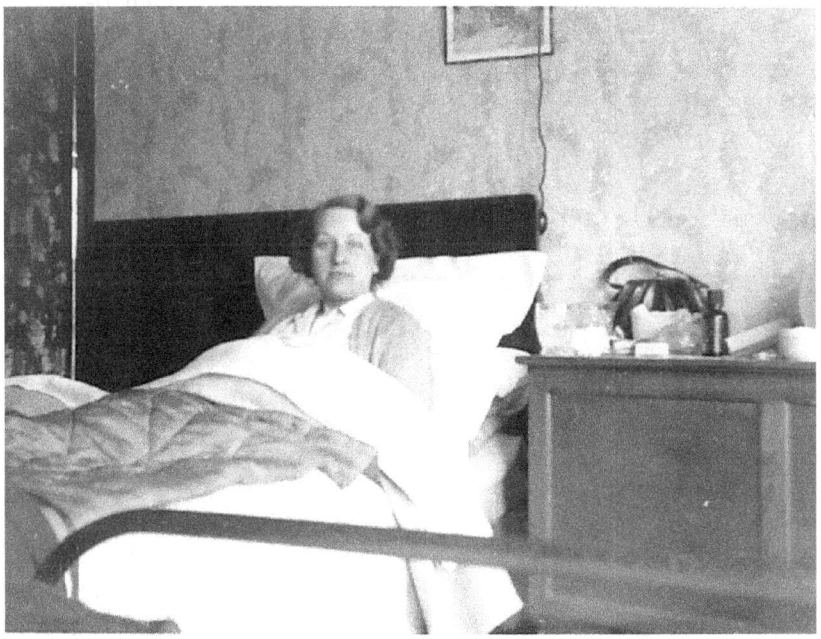

Hilda with whooping cough at Eastbourne Road 1954

Hilary was born at Alice's house on 22nd May 1954, a few weeks earlier than planned. Victor had been tipped off that something was about to happen and arranged a day off work from Hindson's. He turned up at Eastbourne Road on his motorcycle in good time for the birth.

Christine remembers him bringing her new sister downstairs, and her father holding her in the air shouting, 'It's a girl!' To mark the occasion, Victor bought Hilda a gold watch, which is now with Hilary for safe keeping.

Alice, Allan and Marion were delighted to be asked if they would take on the role of God parents for Hilary, and she was christened at St. Barnabas Church.

With Hilda recovering from her cracked rib, Christine still getting over peritonitis, and a new baby to look after it was decided that they would stay at Alice's until everything settled down. There was little point in Victor travelling between the empty cottage at Ravenside and Hindsons each day, so he rented a room at 22 Cheltenham Terrace in Heaton, Newcastle. The family returned to Ravenside at the end of the summer, in time for Christine to start the 1954/55 year at Chopwell School.

Always looking to better his position, in July 1953 Victor asked Hindsons to give him a reference, but it was May 1954 before he applied to Simson Shand Limited, a print company in Hertford. Although nothing resulted from that application, the company wrote to him in October 1954 asking if he was still interested in a position. As well as an attractive wage with the offer of substantial overtime, the company also included a house in Harlow New Town as part of the offer, and free transport between Harlow and Hertford each day. Victor decided to stay at Hindsons.

Just as the family were preparing for Christmas, Victor received the news that his father had suffered a serious heart attack and had died on 20th December 1954 at Stockport Infirmary. Although he and his father had parted on the worst of terms, Victor attended the funeral and re-established contact with his step-mother and the rest of his family.

Unsurprisingly, since Ravenside Cottage was in such a rural setting, there are many tales to be told associated with animals.

Hilda's brother Allan was visiting one day and he, Victor and Christine took a stroll around the field behind the cottage. Out of the blue, a pig appeared through the farm fence. It galloped across to Christine, knocked her over, and started rolling on her legs. Victor and Allan ran to help with Victor waving a walking stick and shouting 'Get off! Get off!' The pig scrambled up and ran back towards the farm, grunting as it went. Christine was none the worse for the experience and still loves pigs.

The walk to Chopwell school took Hilda and Christine across a number of fields, and it was not unusual for some to have grazing cattle. On one occasion, they had walked across what appeared to be an empty field, and just as they climbed over a stile they heard the thunder of hooves growing steadily louder. Turning in the direction of the sound, they saw a young man being chased by a bullock. He just made it to the edge of the field and cleared a five bar gate with height to spare.

One afternoon Victor heard a dog barking in the distance. That was not particularly unusual, but it continued on and off for almost two days, so he and Christine went to see what was going on. The barking was coming from a nearby wood, and they found a dog trapped inside a brick-walled circular structure which looked as though it was made to hold water. It was dry, though, and Victor managed to climb inside, grab the dog, and push it over the wall. The dog ran off, never to be seen again.

Towards the end of summer 1953, Victor was keeping the cottage garden in shape. As usual Christine was helping out, when Victor turned over some soil and discovered a wasps' ground nest. The wasps were less than happy at being disturbed and swarmed around Christine, who was badly stung. Hilda treated the stings with a Reckitt's 'blue bag'. One of these was more usually added to the laundry to give whites a blue tinge. As well as synthetic ultramarine it contained baking soda, which being alkaline counteracted the acidic wasp venom. Hilda soaked the blue bag and rubbed it over each of the stings, taking away the pain.

Chopwell railway terminus, Ravenside garden, Hilda and Christine, Christine with Sandy and Smudge

Not all the animal tales ended happily. The family dog, Sandy, was out one day for a walk with Victor and Christine in woodland behind the cottage when she suddenly collapsed. Victor carried her home, but the dog had eaten poison and died before they could seek any treatment. Later, when Hilda was passing a slice of filled sponge across the tea table, the layer fell open like a dog's mouth. 'Dead dog,' said Christine, remembering how Sandy had looked when Victor carried her home.

Restoring contact with his step-mother turned out to be a mistake, and her dislike for Hilda again began to cause problems. Victor applied for a cottage in Styford, less than 10 miles west from Ravenside towards Corbridge. Although it was not very far away, he hoped that by not sharing the address he would escape his step-mother's invective.

Styford (1955 - 1956)

After the waters of the North Tyne and South Tyne converge at Hexham, the river winds through the Tyne Valley past Corbridge and Styford on its way to Newcastle and the North Sea some 14 miles downstream.

The small village of Styford survived the onslaught of the Scots and plague in medieval times, but catastrophic flooding in the late 1700s destroyed all but a few cottages. In 1816, any traces of the original village were removed to form the grounds of Styford Hall, a large country house which is now a Grade II listed building. Styford did, however, grow again into a thriving community although even today it has a population of only around 100.

Rarely available, as they were built for agricultural workers on the estate, one of the Styford Hall cottages was vacant and Victor succeeded in renting the cottage to the right in the photograph below.

Styford Hall Cottages

The cottage was very basic with outside toilets, no electricity, heating by way of an open fire downstairs, lighting with Tilly lamps and candles, and cooking by solid fuel. There was no water supply to the cottage until just before the family moved in. The supply was negotiated between the estate office and the agent for the cottage, with one agreeing to pay for the supply to be put in if the other would buy the sink.

In order to secure the cottage, Victor was employed by the Styford Hall Estate at High Barns Farm as a part-time herdsman and part-time gardener. Every third weekend, he had to take over from the full-time herdsman and milk the cows. In addition, he undertook to take charge of the kitchen garden and help out with other jobs on a casual basis. His basic wage was 30 shillings a day plus 2/6d an hour for any casual work. The cottage was free of rent while Victor was employed by the estate, with three months notice required to vacate.

The family moved in on Monday 24th January 1955. The winter of 1955 was very cold, with strong easterly winds bringing heavy snowfall to the north of England. Severe night temperatures and Jack Frost inside the windows meant that some form of heating was required upstairs, and a paraffin heater was kept alight on the landing to keep the worst of the chill from the bedrooms. One bitterly cold night, Hilda was lighting the paraffin heater when it burst into flames without warning. Against all modern day recommendations, she rushed downstairs for a bucket of water and threw it over the heater. Luckily, that was enough to extinguish the flames and no damage was done.

One of the first jobs after the family arrived was to settle Christine into school. The nearest was in Corbridge, about three miles to the east of Styford and Hilda enrolled Christine at Corbridge County Infants School off Princes Street. The distance from Styford Cottages to where the bus stopped on the main Corbridge road is about half a mile, so Hilda walked Christine down to the bus stop and back again in the afternoon after waiting to pick her up. She was only eight years old, and although the world was a much safer place in the 1950s than it is now, it would have been risky letting her go alone.

In the cottage next door, 70 year old Alexander Hindmarsh lived by himself, working as the gamekeeper for Styford Hall. His father William was also a gamekeeper when the family lived at Sod Hall, north of the river in the sprawling village of Stocksfield, before Mr Hindmarsh (which the family always called him, perhaps out of respect for his shotgun) moved to the cottage at Styford. He kept chickens, together with a bad-tempered cockerel. The cottages had outside toilets, and one day when Christine had taken toddler Hilary for a call of nature to the outside toilet, the cockerel ran across and attacked them by jumping up, sharp claws outstretched. Luckily, Mr Hindmarsh heard the commotion and dashed outside, and the girls were able to escape safely back inside the cottage.

Christine and Hilary at Styford 1956, and rear of Styford Hall cottages

One of the advantages of having a gamekeeper live next door was the occasional supply of birds, usually pheasants. Hilda would pluck these and use them for stews or to bake into pies, making extra so there was enough to share with Mr Hindmarsh in return for his generosity.

The family hadn't long moved into their new home, when on 24th March 1955 Victor had a serious accident. He was riding his motor cycle to work in heavy rain along Westgate Road in Newcastle at 7:20am, when a Morris commercial goods van owned by Associated Dairies and Farm Stores turned into his path just past Kingsley Terrace. Victor swerved but, although he was travelling at less than 30mph, was unable to avoid a collision. The side of the van was damaged and the front window was broken.

Westgate Road junction with Kingsley Terrace (present day)

Unlike today, crash helmets were not generally worn and Victor had on a leather cap and goggles. He suffered a depressed fracture of the skull, lacerations, and was knocked out by the impact. An ambulance took him to Newcastle General Hospital where he had an operation on his skull. He had to give up his job as a printer's compositor because of headaches and an inability to concentrate for long periods. Although subject to bouts of irritability, he managed to continue working in the trade, but as a proof reader. That change of job turned out to be significant, because in 1956, Hindson's were looking for a Head Reader. Victor applied for and was offered the new position.

Victor sued Associated Dairies for damages, and on 15th May 1956 the case went before Mr Justice Byrne at Newcastle Assizes where he awarded £1565 damages. That was higher than would normally have been called for, but doctors agreed that there was a real risk of epilepsy in later life. Fortunately that didn't happen.

Just 200 yards or so along the lane leading to the main road to Corbridge, stood High Barns Farm run by the Laws. Hilda was friendly with the family there, and the two daughters Dorothy and Pat Law frequently visited the cottage and joined in with family activities.

High Barns Farm

High Barns Farm dates back to the early 1800s when Styford was a small hamlet of around twelve houses and a population of about 70. It was probably built around the same time as Styford Hall, after the village had been destroyed by flood in 1771. Torrential rain had fallen throughout the 16th November of that year, and continued into the night of the 17th. By about two o'clock in the morning, the Tyne had risen some six feet higher than anyone had known it to and all the bridges in the Tyne Valley were destroyed except, remarkably, the one not far from Styford at Corbridge. By dawn, the whole of Styford was under water and most of the buildings had collapsed beyond any hope of repair. It is reported that following the flood, many of the residents relocated south of the river to Broomhaugh which was less badly hit.

Although the human population flourished as the village was rebuilt, the same could not be said for the rabbits. The area of countryside around Styford was badly hit by the nationwide outbreak of myxomatosis in 1953, which killed tens of millions of rabbits along the length of Britain. Most farmers welcomed the elimination of what was a serious agricultural pest, but the public was horrified to see so many dead and dying animals in the fields.

Hilda (back right), Christine, Hilary and Pat Law at Styford

The lack of rabbits also meant that Judy, the family's pet dog, had none to chase. At first, it was fun seeing her run around and around the two cottages at full pelt, but it wasn't for the lack of rabbits. Judy was having phantom pregnancies, and this was going to become more of a problem as the years passed.

Through working at High Barns Farm at weekends, and occasionally in the evening when he returned from his job at Hindson's, Victor was used to livestock. Luckily, that meant he wasn't fazed when one day the Law's bull escaped and ran down the road between the farm and the cottage just as he and Christine were returning from a walk. Victor threw Christine over the nearest hedge for safety while he helped to turn the bull and send it on its way back to the farm.

Hilda (behind) and Dorothy Law on Victor's motorcycle

Victor's motorcycle accident was to open up a new beginning for the family, because they were able to use the compensation as a deposit for their own house. The local journal had a wide selection of properties in the area, and on 25th June 1956 the shortlist came down to two stone-built cottages. One was a semi-detached house with five rooms on a large plot of land at Busty Bank, Burnopfield, about half distance to Newcastle three miles east of Chopwell. The other was Sealburn Cottage at Greenside, a mile south of Ryton, which was detached with a large garden and ample space for a garage, priced at an eye-catching £1,350.

The family decided on Sealburn Cottage. It had a charming location at the entrance to Sealburn Farm, and was the first cottage seen when approaching Greenside by way of Lead Road. Only half a mile from Greenside village centre, there was easy access to shops, doctors and a school. A reliable and frequent bus service operated from the village to and from Newcastle.

Taking account of expenses following Victor's motorcycle accident they could afford a 50% deposit, and on 30th July 1956 the Halifax Building Society granted a 15 year mortgage for the balance.

Greenside (1956 - 1960)

Sealburn Cottage needed decorating throughout and required a considerable amount of repair, which was probably the reason for the attractive purchase price. When they realised there was so much work needed it was not too late to pull out of the purchase, but the family had fallen in love with the property. The keys were made available on 28th August 1956 prior to completion of the purchase contract, after the seller's solicitors agreed that Hilda and Victor could take possession in order to make the cottage suitable to move into. Some of the repairs required were substantial, starting with a new chimney and leaking roof. This work was carried out the day before the family moved in on 9th October 1956, but must have been rushed because major damp problems surfaced the following year.

Sealburn Cottage, Greenside 1958 with Singer Super 10 in driveway

Victor and Hilda struck up a friendship with Albert and Marian Pyrah, who lived not far away at 71 Rockwood Hill Estate. Their children, Frank and Robbie, were great pals with Christine although Hilary was still very young. The four of them were often found playing in the garden, and Christine and Frank would spend hours on end in the open cast pits opposite the cottage.

In February 1957 a rogue flu virus broke out in Singapore, and by the summer it had spread to epidemic proportions and reached all corners of the world.

Christened 'Asian Flu', it was first reported in England in late June, and by the end of the year some ten million people in Great Britain were estimated to have contracted the virus with some 14,000 dying. Affected most were those between five and forty years of age, and in London some 110,000 children were off school with Asian Flu.

Although Hilda, Victor and Hilary managed to avoid the virus, Christine caught it and was bedridden for two weeks with a high fever, aches and pains, weakness, and a nasty cough.

During the winter of 1957/58, damp patches appeared in one of the bedrooms and the lounge. A builder suggested that these were partly due to damage to one of the chimneys and to loose pointing on the gable ends. The work was completed in May, but the damp problem remained. Victor examined the repairs closely and complained that not only were there parts of the re-pointing which had not been properly finished, the whole of the top of the east gable wall was still to be done. The builder agreed to put things right and returned in the summer, but the pointing continued to be an issue and Victor refused to pay that element of the bill until everything was put right. Letters were sent from both sides, and It was October 1960 after the family had moved to their next house in Kempston before the dispute was eventually settled.

The motorcycle was ideal for travelling to and from Newcastle for work, but less so for taking the family on outings. Victor bought a 1939 Singer Super 10 saloon in 1958. Although nearly 20 years old, it was a relatively modern design with an overhead cam 10 horsepower engine and two electric windscreen wipers which replaced the single vacuum-powered wiper on the previous model.

Pet dog Judy's phantom pregnancies were becoming more difficult to handle. In the early summer of 1958 she made a place for herself on an old chair in one of the outhouse buildings at the rear of the house where Victor kept his motorcycle. Judy became very protective of her area, and on one occasion when Victor went in to get his motorcycle out, she reacted viciously. The vet said it would be best for everyone if she was put to sleep. Christine, of course, was very much against that idea but Victor and the vet came up with a plan.

Hilary had turned four in May 1958, and old enough to appreciate a holiday away. They decided on Scotland, although only just over the border at Eyemouth. A caravan was booked for 16th - 22nd August at Northburn Caravan Site costing £6.10s.0d. for the week.

Christine often walked their cat Snowy on a lead, so he accompanied the family on the holiday. Judy was left in kennels, and Victor took her away the day before they left. That just left Frank and Robbie Pyrah to feed and water the black and white Dutch rabbit each day.

The whole trip was only about 80 miles, so the family took a small detour on the way to Eyemouth to drop in to see Mrs. Wilson. They had moved from Benton in Newcastle some years before, but Mr Lewis had since died.

At the Wilson's on the way to Eyemouth with Snowy, and Hilda with Mrs. Wilson

Eyemouth is so named because it is situated at the mouth of the Eye, curiously not called a river, but 'Eye Water'. It is a quaint fishing town with a safe harbour, and narrow streets lined with 17th century houses reminding visitors of the smuggling days of the past. At each side of the town the landscape rises up over high cliffs dropping to sandy coves which look out to deep clear water.

Caravan at Eyemouth, with a young girl from a neighbouring caravan

There was to be some bad news after the family returned home. Victor went to collect Judy from the kennels but said that she had accidentally been given to someone else while they were away. It would be many years later that Christine discovered Judy had actually been taken to the vet and put to sleep the day before they had gone away.

The family sorely missed having a dog around the house, and towards the end of 1958 Victor took Christine to see a litter of boxer puppies. With great difficulty she chose one, christened her Beava, and the puppy was bought for her as a Christmas present.

Beava, Hilda, Hilary, Christine, Frank and Robbie Pyrah at Sealburn Cottage

There is little doubt that Victor was highly respected at Hindsons. In 1957, Victor was given 25 ordinary shares in the company, which paid a small dividend. Although he held the shares for a number of years, by 1973 the dividend had dwindled to pennies, so Victor sold them.

At Hindson's 21st Annual Dinner held at the Crown Hotel in Newcastle on 18th January 1958, Victor was called upon to make a small speech and raise a toast to the company after the chairman's opening toast and remarks. The following year, Victor was charged with making the arrangements for the dinner which turned out to be a great success.

After buying the Singer, Victor designed and built a garage to the left of the cottage. It measured 16 feet long by 8 feet wide, was 7 feet high to the eaves and 10 feet to the roof ridge. The plan was to include a concrete floor the following summer, but in the meantime it was left as compacted earth. Access to the garage was along the entrance lane to Sealburn Farm, then across the front of the cottage.

Car ownership in the 1950s was nothing like it is today. Servicing was a frequent requirement, and almost all owners carried out tasks such as changing the oil, checking the fluid levels, adding grease to steering joints and making repairs. Most cars were unreliable, and the Singer was no exception. On one occasion the gearbox required major work, and Victor, with the help of Albert Pyrah, stripped it down and rebuilt it. On another, the rear springs needed replacing and Victor and Albert carried out that repair as well. Christine remembers her father taking everyone, including all the Pyrah family, for a test drive around the country lanes.

Victor with the Singer Super 10

It transpired that there was no legal right of access via the lane to Sealburn Farm. This meant a new access was required to the garage from the frontage of the property. Victor, as always with help from Albert Pyrah, created a new access point through the front hedge. Although traffic was much lighter than it is today, they inset the gate to allow the Singer to drive off the road and stop without interfering with vehicles travelling along Lead Road.

During negotiations around the sale of the cottage, a question was raised concerning vehicles driving across the footpath, which must not have occurred to Victor when he installed the front access. Durham County Council deemed that this work had to be completed before the cottage could be sold. A dropped kerb was built by the local council at Victor's expense in April 1959.

Victor's father Cuthbert had died six years previously, his birth mother Lily drowned when he was four years old, and his only living full blood relative, his younger sister Yvonne, led a very troubled life in and out of mental institutions. After leaving Styford without telling the family where they were going, there had been no contact with his half-siblings since moving to Greenside. In 1959 Victor's step-mother Hannah tracked him down. She had previously written disturbing letters intended to create tension between Victor and Hilda, and Victor was sure she would begin to do so again. There seemed to be only one way to be free of the family pressures, and that was to move far away from the area.

Victor and Hilda scoured the press for vacancies in the printing trade, and found a small concern in Kempston, near Bedford, about fifty miles north of London. The Sidney Press was advertising for a reader, which was exactly the position that Victor was looking for.

Sealburn Cottage was put up for sale, and quickly made the asking price of £1450. After ten years with the company, Victor tendered his resignation to Hindson's who furnished him with a glowing reference. He formally left the company at the end of May, although he was allowed leave to go early in order to make arrangements for accommodation at his new place of work.

Kempston (1960 - 1963)

Victor's new job with The Sidney Press included not only removal expenses to the area, but also the option to rent one of the houses owned by the company. There were many arrangements to be made, so Victor travelled to Bedford alone at the end of April 1960. He rented a flat at 55 Shakespeare Road, a large semidetached Victorian house in Bedford's 'Poets' area and a stone's throw from The Sidney Press in Sidney Road.

By 10th May, Victor had arranged to rent a three bedroom house at 3 King William Close in Kempston. He set the move in motion straight away, and booked a removal firm, A.C. Farmer, for 16th June. Their estimate for moving all the furniture and belongings from Greenside to Kempston was £48.14s.0d, a bill which would be paid by The Sidney Press.

3 King William Close (left, now reassigned as number 5)

When the family moved in, there were only eight semi-detached houses in the close and they were numbered sequentially clockwise from one to eight. The housing explosion since then has seen the number of houses in the close grow to nearly 40 and the numbering was altered to a more conventional 'odds and evens' system. This means that the family home at number 3, the third house on the left entering the close and the left-most house in the photograph, has been reassigned the number 5.

Before leaving Hindson's, Hilda and Victor had discussed what should be done about the pension fund built up with the company. It was not a huge amount, and they decided it would be more useful for them to have the cash in hand rather than salt it away until retirement. So Victor requested a refund of pension payments made to Hindon's pension fund, and a cheque for £123.19s.9d arrived at his flat in Shakespeare Road on 24th May 1960.

On 13th June, Victor hired a car in Bedford and drove the 230 miles or so to Greenside to help with packing and final arrangements for leaving Sealburn Cottage. Hilda had already done much of the work, but with only three days to go there was still plenty to get finished.

The furniture van turned up mid-morning on Thursday 16th June. The removal men didn't take long to load up the boxes and furniture, and just after lunch the van set off on its journey to Kempston with Hilda, Victor, Christine and Hilary following behind in the rented car. Although the weather was warm, it was raining steadily in Greenside but by the time the convoy reached Lincolnshire the rain had stopped and the sun appeared from behind the grey clouds.

Arriving in Kempston around teatime, the contents of the removal van were promptly transferred to the house. Although the furniture was placed more or less in the correct rooms, the boxes of belongings and household items were dumped anywhere there was space for them. Everybody was hungry and tired after the long journey, but there was to be no cooking on the first night and there would be much unpacking to be done before the kitchen was ready for use. The family drove into Bedford and enjoyed a special Chinese meal at the recently opened Pearl of Hong Kong restaurant on The Broadway.

Hilda, Hilary and Christine at King William Close

Although Kempston was a small town in the 1960s, it grew out of a rural parish made up of a number of hamlets called 'Ends': Up End, Bell End, Wood End, Box End and Church End. Each 'End' had its own school, so there was no shortage when it came to choosing one for Christine and Hilary.

    Christine had turned 13 a couple of months before the move and was enrolled at Robert Bruce Middle School. This school began as Kempston Senior Council School in 1928 becoming, successively, Kempston County Secondary Modern, Robert Bruce County Secondary Modern and finally in 1960, Robert Bruce Middle School. At six years old, Hilary was too young to attend Robert Bruce, and had a longer walk than Christine to Up End school which took mixed pupils between the ages of four and seven years. After two years at Up End, she moved on to Balliol Primary School, which was about the same distance but in a different direction.

With the children at school all day, and Victor working long shifts at The Sidney Press, Hilda decided to take a part time job. A local grocery store manager, Mrs. Brown, was looking for someone to handle the accounts of customers placing orders for delivery, and with Hilda being good with figures, record keeping and organisation the job was an ideal match. The store, now St. John Food & Wine, was in St. John's Street on the way to Up End School, so within easy walking distance. Hilda had no trouble making up the boxes for delivery, writing out the sales slips and keeping the ledgers up to date in between looking after the family.

Victor at King William Close with Hilda and Hilary, 1960

Television broadcasts had started in the mid 1930s, but were suspended in 1939 for the years of the Second World War and resumed in June 1946. The broadcasting of the coronation of Queen Elizabeth II in 1953 led to a sharp increase in the popularity of television sets and the introduction of commercial broadcasting in 1955 sent demand even higher. By 1959, 60% of households owned a television and on 31st August 1960 Hilda and Victor bought a Murphy V530 Television/Radio combination set from Weatherheads in Bedford for £74.11s.0d.

Murphy V530 television, c1960

To say the set was unreliable would be an understatement. It went into Weatherheads' workshop for repairs fifteen times between 1961 and 1966. Over the years, they replaced various valves, mains transformer, volume control, rectifier, turret tuner, line output transformer, discriminator transformer, over-heated resistors, oscillator coil, and HT rectifier. Almost everything appears to have been replaced except for the tube.

Hilda and Victor loved classical music, and had a large collection of books about composers and their music. Hilda bought Victor a copy of *Conductor's Gallery* by Donald Brook for their first wedding anniversary in 1947. They often listened to the BBC Light Programme on the radio and played a collection of 78 r.p.m. records on a home-made wind-up gramophone. New recordings had become widely available on modern records which the gramophone was unable to play, and a new record player was on the cards. Christmas 1960 saw a large present under the tree for Christine, which turned out to be a Philips stereophonic record player. Although probably not part of the plan, the record player usually found its way into Christine's bedroom to play her Elvis Presley, Bobby Vee, Neil Sedaka and Dion discs!

Christine's record player, and in her bedroom

Also prompted by their interest in music, Victor bought a second-hand upright Steck piano from Thomas Fraser's shop on the corner of Harpur Street and Tavistock Street in Bedford. Christine began taking piano lessons from Phyllis Chance, who lived locally at 16 Lodge Avenue in Kempston, and became quite proficient at playing popular pieces composed by Beethoven and Bach. She continued with the lessons for about two years until around the time she started work, at which point Hilary took over. Hilary became skilful as well, taking examinations and reaching Grade 2 in The Associated Board of The Royal Schools of Music in 1963. She also played in front of a large audience, which included Hilda and Victor, at the 1963 Bedford Festival of Music. The festival was founded in 1921 to showcase the talents of young people in Bedfordshire, and is still held annually during the first week of March at the Corn Exchange in Bedford.

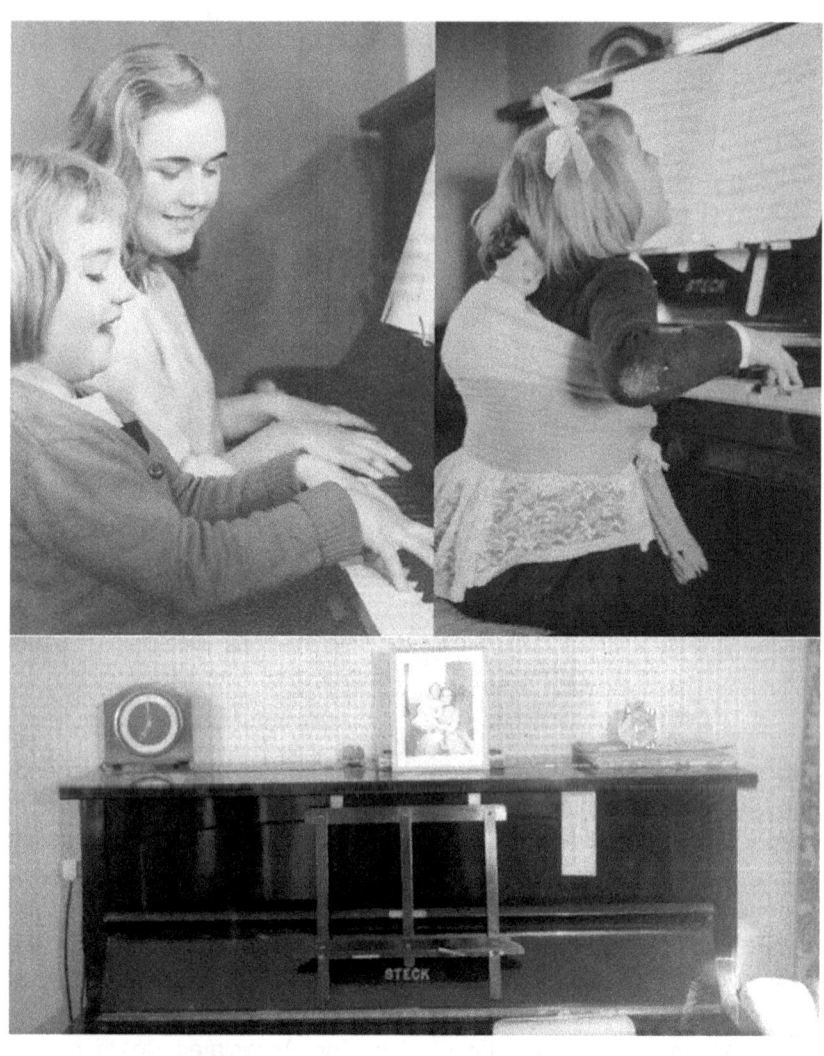

Christine and Hilary at the piano, c1961

His career in the printing trade had given Victor a good eye for everything artistic. He had a talent for drawing and painting and took up photography. Unlike the present day, when everyone has a sophisticated phone camera at their fingertips and software which can turn the most lacklustre snap into a sparkling example of photographic imagery, in the 1960s good cameras were both expensive and difficult to use.

Taking the pictures was only half the total experience, and processing the images was an essential part of any photographer's skill base. Also, although colour photography was invented in 1907, in the 1960s colour film was very expensive, as was commercial processing of colour prints. For the amateur photographer, who would usually print images on large sheets of paper, the cost was a major prohibitive factor. So Victor, like most of his cohort, used black and white film and processed black and white prints. Since the vast majority of humans see in colour, producing images in monochrome presented a further challenge to perfect the reproduction of tonal range with only black, white, and shades of grey at the photographer's disposal.

Victor bought a number of cameras while living in Kempston. These included a TLR (twin lens reflex) Rolleicord, a Periflex II with 1.9mm lens, and an Ensign Auto-range camera. He also purchased a flash gun, a tripod, and some large reflectors, spotlights and bulb holders from which made his own set of studio lights. The bathroom was converted to a darkroom by making foldable work surfaces and light-proof blinds for the window, and finally a photographic enlarger, safe light, developer tank, sets of dishes and a range of chemicals and papers for processing prints completed his purchases.

As well as taking photographs in and around Kempston and Bedford, Victor also turned his hand to portrait photography and took on projects such as recording events at parties, charity walks and special occasions drawing the line only when it came to weddings which he felt were too much of a responsibility.

Although he never entered any of his photographs for competitions or sought publication, much of his work would have received enthusiastic acclaim.

After a busy year settling into a new way of life, the family booked a chalet for between 20th and 27th May 1961 near Burnham-on-Sea on the north Somerset coast. Although West Country holidays were already popular in the 1960s, that part of the country was still more peaceful and easy-going than the Bedford area. The Knoll & Midwarren Caravan Park at Brean Sands where they stayed is squashed between the western tip of the Mendip Hills surrounding the awesome Cheddar Gorge, and the soft sands alongside the Bristol Channel. The log cabin was basic but comfortable, the countryside offered beautiful walks and the beaches were clean and welcoming. The only downside to the holiday was that Christine developed a large boil on the back of her knee which refused to respond to basic treatment from the local chemist.

Somerset holiday, May 1961

Shortly after moving to Kempston, Hilda had begun to feel something was not quite right with her health but put it down to the upheaval and change of lifestyle. She was having trouble sleeping and lost a lot of weight. Rather than recharge her batteries, the holiday in Somerset brought things to a head when she realised she had far less energy than usual. A trip to the doctor returned a diagnosis of hyperthyroidism, confirmed by a noticeable swelling of the thyroid gland in her neck.

Hilda, prior to thyroid operation, 1962

Faced with a choice between hormone treatment, radiotherapy, and surgery, Hilda decided to wait and see how the condition developed. By the spring of 1962, she realised that something had to be done and opted for an operation to remove most of her thyroid gland.

The operation was carried out at Bedford General Hospital in August 1962, and after recovering sufficiently Hilda was moved to the Homewood Convalescent Home at Aspley Heath, near Bletchley. Built in the late 1800s as a school, the building was purchased by Bedford County Council in 1919 on condition that a covenant restricting its use to a private residence be lifted. It was converted and used as a convalescent home for the County Hospital between the wars and during the Second World War was used as a refuge for children who had been evacuated. In the late 1940s the building was enlarged to accommodate 22 patients. No operations or medical treatments were carried out at Homewood; it was only used for people who needed a quiet retreat to aid recovery following illness or surgery.

Hilda made a lot of friends during her stay, who kept in touch by letter after she left. She had a surprise one day when fifteen year old Christine took Hilary, who was just eight, to see her unannounced. They had caught a bus into town from Kempston, then another out to Aspley Guise. By the end of September Hilda had regained sufficient strength to return home.

Homewood convalescent home

Christine left Robert Bruce school at the end of the 1962 spring term after she had turned 15, the usual school leaving age until it was raised to 16 from 1964 onwards. A job as receptionist at the solicitors offices of Conquest Clare & Binns at 30 Mill Street in Bedford town centre was advertised and Christine applied for the position. After an interview with the firm's senior partners she was offered the post, working in the front office. There were about ten solicitors and legal practitioners working in the building, offering services such as conveyancing, divorce, wills, and contracts as well as legal representation in court, so Christine was kept busy with members of the public attending appointments throughout the day.

Victor decided to change jobs. He applied to E.J. Day on Clapham Road in 1962 and was taken on as a reader. He had no idea that the son of the print room manager, John Wadner, would turn out to provide an interesting turn of events a few years later.

After renting a house provided by Sidney Press in Kempston for nearly three years, Victor and Hilda were able to consider buying another house but remembering the problems with the property they purchased at Greenside, they were keen not to put themselves in that position again. In 1953, a huge property development was initiated on the east side of Bedford across farmland between Putnoe Lane and Church Lane. Around 7000 houses were planned, together with convenient shopping precincts at the Goldington end of the estate and centrally at Queens Drive.

A house in Cotswold Close, a quiet cul-de-sac, came up for auction with W. & H. Peacock in early December 1962. It was only a few minutes' walk from the Queens Drive shops, a newly built public house The Queens Tavern, local police station, and doctor's surgery. At the same time, another house became available at 7 Fosterhill Road near the centre of Bedford. Victor and Hilda made appointments to view both houses on 6th December, Cotswold Close at 5.30pm and Fosterhill Road at 7pm.

They quickly decided that the house in Fosterhill Road was older than they wanted, so chose the house in Cotswold Close. The price was £2,975 which was rather more than they planned to pay, but it was almost new, having been built by Wimpey only three years previously. That should mean they would save on renovation and ongoing repair costs. They offered the full price, and this was accepted by the seller who agreed to proceed without delay. The Bedfordshire Building Society advanced £2,700 at a monthly repayment cost of £18.9s.0d.

Cotswold Close (1963 - 1971)

The winter of 1963 was the coldest on record since 1740 when George II was on the throne and Sir Robert Walpole was Prime Minister. A high pressure system moved across the country just before Christmas 1962, pulling bitterly cold winds down from the Arctic. Snowfall began in Scotland on Christmas Eve giving Glasgow its first white Christmas since before the Second World War, and by Boxing Day a foot of snow had covered the whole of the British Isles. By the end of the year some areas had snowdrifts twenty feet deep, roads and railways were blocked, telephone and power lines down, and towns and villages were cut off for days at a time.

Victor, Hilda, Christine and Hilary moved into 30 Cotswold Close on 18th January 1963. That same day, a temperature of minus 22.2°C was recorded in Scotland. Although Bedford was not as bad as that, the average temperature was well below freezing for the whole of January and in February, nearby Woburn recorded a minimum temperature of minus 21°C.

30 Cotswold Close, Bedford, 1995

On arrival at their new home, the family was greeted by Jack Frost on the inside of all the windows and after turning on the water supply discovered that the pipes were frozen solid. There were not going to be any hot cups of tea for quite a while.

Setting up the new house turned out to be more expensive than was first thought, and Hilda decided she would find a job to help out towards the mortgage. She had excellent training in book keeping prior to her time in the ATS and plenty of experience looking after the shop accounts in Kempston. She applied for a job at Proper Pride Ltd. a lingerie and hosiery manufacturer in Windsor Road, Bedford in their accounting department. Starting on 11th March 1963, Hilda was given charge of the bought ledger, responsible for recording all goods coming into the company. There were no computers in use at the time, so the ledger was hand written and the accounts balanced using a basic mechanical calculator.

Hilda at Proper Pride

Getting to her new job each day was a long journey, and meant catching a bus into the town centre, and another to her place of work. Had they wished to, the neighbours could have accurately checked their clocks as Hilda walked quickly along the close at precisely the same time each morning, down the alley to Queens Drive, and arrived just in time where her bus stopped at the local shops.

The new house brought with it some new excitement. Christine had been seeing a young trainee architect who worked across the road from her office at Conquest Clare and Binns for some time, and just before Christine's sixteenth birthday they decided to become engaged to be married. Although Peter's mother handled the catering arrangements for the engagement party, which was held at Cotswold Close, there was still a great deal of work for Hilda to do especially as it was only a few weeks after moving in. The relationship dwindled after three years or so, and the engagement was called off.

Victor wanted to continue his photography hobby and shortly after moving in purchased an Asahi Pentax Single Lens Reflex camera for £132, and a Petriflex 7 with a wide angle lens for £140. Then, much to Hilda's chagrin, he suggested he could convert the bathroom in the same way he had at King William Close. He re-jigged the collapsible work area he had made at Kempston to fit the different sized bath, but before he got around to making a light-tight shutter for the window decided that with three females in the house, putting the bathroom out of action for hours on end might not be such a great idea.

So Victor's attention turned to the attic. He laid a wooden floor over part of the area, and built some shelves and work surfaces to take his enlarger and developing dishes. Everybody was happy, and Victor would disappear into the attic for entire evenings producing fabulous photographs in his makeshift darkroom.

Apparently photography was not Victor's only pastime, and over the years he would often retreat to the space in the attic but no photographs would appear. He eventually told the family that he was writing a book, which would be published under the pseudonym of Edward Sears. Although the manuscript was hungrily awaited, it never saw the light of day. Nobody knew what the book was about and, mysteriously, the manuscript has never been found.

Beava quickly settled into life in the new house, and was friends with everyone, humans and animals alike. She soon found her way around the local area, and would take herself 200 yards or so down the road for a wee on a nearby green if no-one was available to go with her. She loved Hilary's pet budgerigar Santy and was happy to let him sit on her head.

Beava, photographed by Victor

Although Beava had been very healthy over the years, in 1964 she suddenly became ill and was diagnosed with pyometra, a serious womb infection. It is not uncommon in female unneutered dogs, yet very difficult to treat without resorting to aggressive surgery. One morning Hilda had gone out to the local shops leaving Christine alone with Beava, when the dog lurched from the chair where she was resting and died just as Hilda returned. The family were grief-stricken. Beava had been a wonderful pet who was no trouble at all, as well as being a link back to country life in Greenside.

Heating and hot water at Cotswold Close was provided by an open fire in the front room and immersion heater, and after suffering two very cold winters, in 1965 it was time to get a proper heating system installed. Hilda liked to see a proper fire rather than the gas fires which were becoming common in the sixties, so they decided to have a Parkray solid fuel burner. This heated the water, although an immersion heater was retained for use during the summer months, and two radiators upstairs.

Although Hilda's other siblings did not visit Cotswold Close, Florrie and Bob, with their poodle Fifi, travelled down on the bus a couple of times to stay a few nights. Five minutes' walk from the house, down to the end of the close and through an alleyway, stood The Queens Tavern and everyone would walk down for an evening of drinks.

Florrie, Fifi, Hilda and Hilary at Cotswold Close, 1968

Since moving from Greenside, the family could not afford to run a car so had been over eight years using public transport and bicycles to get around. Victor changed jobs again for more pay, and in the summer of 1968 was back working shifts at Sidney Press. On 16th September that year Victor purchased a Morris 1000 6cwt van in 'Baltic Blue', registration 520NBM, from Kennings in Bedford for £95. Although useful for carrying goods, the van was less convenient when the whole family needed to go somewhere together. Victor had fitted two seats in the load area of the van, but they were difficult to access and gave a limited view of the road ahead. This was prone to making a back seat passenger a little dizzy since all they could see was the tarmac rushing beneath the bonnet.

Although Hilda and Victor rarely went to the Queens Tavern by themselves, Christine and Hilary often popped into the off license for a bottle of Merrydown Cider, cigarettes, or in Hilary's case, packets of crisps. One evening in June 1969, Victor walked into the public bar with Christine and ordered a pint and a Cherry B. Phil Wadner worked behind the bar and in the off license most evenings and had been quietly smitten with Christine for some time. That same evening they arranged to meet after the pub closed, and never looked back.

One evening in the late summer of 1969, Victor asked whether Christine and Phil would like to go out for a drink at The Wellington public house on Bedford Road towards Kempston. There was to be some guitar playing and singing taking place. The evening went well, and Phil played along on guitar for a few of the songs. Halfway home though, with Christine and Phil sitting high up in the back of the van and the woozy effect of the restricted view of the road ahead, Phil let loose with most of the beer he had drunk during the evening. Luckily he missed Hilda, and except for some serious embarrassment, no damage was done which couldn't be cleared up with a bucket and cloth. It was not long afterwards that the van was traded in.

The Morris van had only been with the family just over a year when on 31st December 1969 Victor purchased a Morris 1000 saloon, registration 261CNV, from Holland's Motors in Bedford, trading in the van for £75.

Hilda's commute to work was much easier after buying their own vehicle, as Victor was able to drive her to and from Proper Pride when he was working an appropriate shift. Not wishing to return to using the bus, Hilda split the cost of a taxi with a couple of friends from work when

Victor was not available. They had a standing arrangement with the driver, who always had a good supply of sweets from the Meltis factory in Bedford which he was happy to share with Hilda and her friends. They assumed that one of his other regular fares worked there and took advantage of the free sweets that Meltis handed out to its employees, passing some on to the cab driver each day. There was never a shortage of New Berry Fruits, Turkish Delight, and chocolate liqueurs as well as Chocolat-Tobler products manufactured for the United Kingdom such as Toblerone.

On 20th February 1970, Hilda had a surprise visit at her place of work from Victor, who in turn should have been asleep since he was working a night shift that particular week. Christine had returned home at lunchtime and announced that she and her boyfriend Phil had been married that morning at Bedford Register Office. It was probably not a massive bolt from the blue as there was a high expectation that the couple were to wed, but the news caused much elation and excitement. Christine and Phil paid a short visit to his parents' to break the news, then drove to meet up with Hilda and Victor for a celebration at The Engine and Tender in Midland Road, a stone's throw from the Register Office.

Phil had been sleeping at Cotswold Close for a few nights prior to the wedding, because his grandmother was ill and was staying in his room at home. Hilda took the extra mouth to feed in her stride, as she did most things, and really not much altered after the wedding other than there were fewer sheets to wash. Christine and Phil were rarely at home since Phil worked quite a distance away in Stevenage, and Christine never returned for lunch. The couple were out most evenings, so it was mostly the sleeping arrangements and breakfast that saw much in the way of change.

Phil's car, a rather posh black Vauxhall Victor FB, broke down in a big way two weeks after the wedding. A vehicle was needed urgently and Victor drove Phil to a garage he knew at Marston Moretaine to see if they had anything suitable in stock. The only vehicle ready to go was a blue 1962 Austin A35 van, marked up at £30. A quick test drive later, the money was handed over and Phil drove the van back to Cotswold Close. It was a bit of a letdown after the Vauxhall, which had plush upholstery and a very comfortable ride, but it would only be a temporary measure.

Having an extra car in the drive caused some minor inconvenience, because Victor worked shifts and although there was room for two or more cars in the driveway and at the side of the house, inevitably they were parked in the wrong order. Over the space of a few days Victor built a paved track across the front garden between the driveway and the lounge window so that the van could be parked there, allowing his Morris 1000 to move freely in and out at odd times of the day and night.

It was not long before Christine and Phil decided they wanted to live in a place of their own, and moved out on 6th June 1970 to a flat in Clapham Road, the other side of town. Although the flat had basic furnishings, Hilda and Victor generously helped out with missing items including a brand new bedroom suite.

It had been a long time since the family had been on holiday, and in the summer of 1970 Hilda, Victor and Hilary set off for a week in Bala, a small town in southern Snowdonia. They stayed in a static caravan on Cyffdy Farm about three miles out of town.

Bala is situated close to the largest natural lake in Wales, Llyn Tegid, some four and a half miles long and a mile across at its widest point. A narrow gauge railway runs along the east shore between Bala and Llanuwchllyn offering beautiful views across the lake and the surrounding mountains.

Not only did Bala offer many sights to see and activities to get involved in, it was not far from the heart of Snowdonia and the beautiful Welsh coast. About twenty miles west, and less than a half hour drive away, is the historic town of Harlech and the sumptuous beaches that line Cardigan Bay. To the north west and at a similar distance rises Snowdon, the highest mountain in Wales.

The caravan was located on a sheep farm, so there were quite a few collies running loose which were used to manage the flocks. Victor mentioned to the farmer that they were thinking of buying a dog as a family pet, and at the end of the week a neighbouring farmer turned up with a collie puppy. Apparently it was not thought to have the qualities needed for rounding up sheep, but would make an excellent pet. As soon as the family set eyes on the puppy, there was no going back and he made the trip home sitting next to Hilary on the back seat of the car. They named him Cyffdy, after the farm where they stayed.

Caravan holiday at Bala, 1970

Hilda was not very interested in cars, but Victor had been hankering after something with rather better performance than the Morris 1000. On 3rd February 1971 he purchased a 1964 Triumph Vitesse registration number AEW 65B from Fairway Motors, Tavistock Place for £295. Not only was the engine size 1596cc, but it had six cylinders which made it very smooth as well as much more powerful than the Morris. What Victor liked most about the car was that from the side and back it looked much the same as a standard Triumph Herald, and the only external feature that belied the power hidden under the bonnet was the dual headlamp arrangement. Much to Hilda's dismay, Victor took great delight at pulling away quickly at traffic lights and leaving other unsuspecting cars at some distance behind.

At around the same time, Hilary had turned 17, left school and was working at Bedfordshire County Council. She had completed her training period, moving around all the different departments at the council, and ended up under Social Services in the Welfare Department checking out facilities and care homes for the elderly and children. She had a taste of driving the Morris 1000 before getting her driving licence on the beaches when they were on holiday in Wales, and was learning to drive properly with a mix of lessons from Victor and a local driving school. She was very keen to have a car of her own. Fairway Motors had offered Victor £150 for the Morris in part exchange when he purchased the Vitesse. It was in excellent condition, had been looked after with no expense spared, and was probably worth far more than the part exchange price. It seemed a sensible option to transfer ownership to Hilary instead of trading it in.

Although Hilda had grown used to not having Christine at home, there were still plenty of opportunities for meeting up as the flat was only a fifteen minutes or so drive from Cotswold Close. Christine would often take the bus over there and perhaps do some washing or cleaning, or sometimes take Cyffdy for a short walk to do his business, before Hilda arrived home from work.

Phil, though, was finding travelling from Bedford to Stevenage each day by car quite wearing. His job entailed a long day and most mornings he left Bedford around 5-30am and didn't arrive home until 7pm. The travelling was also expensive because the van was not very economical and used an exorbitant amount of oil for each journey. It was part exchanged at Willington Garage for a Ford Anglia with a more modern engine. Even so, the commute took a lot of hours out of each day and in March 1971 Christine and Phil moved to Stevenage. Phil had reached the end of his apprenticeship with International Computers Limited, and as part of the deal for him to continue working for them they allocated him one of their houses. Stevenage New Town was only twenty years into its development, and most large companies had a housing allocation to attract staff to the area.

Victor was beginning to get itchy feet again, and he and Hilda discussed moving from Cotswold Close. Christine had moved to Stevenage, and Hilary was grown up and probably would soon be considering her future. For some years Victor had been fighting the local council to have ball games banned from a patch of unused land at the bottom of the garden. He made the mistake of telling off the children who were constantly asking for their ball to be returned, and they retaliated by climbing over the garden fence and causing trouble when they knew he was not at home.

In the summer of 1971, a new residential development was announced comprising five large four bedroom detached houses in Goldington to the east of the town. Hilda particularly liked the idea of the fitted kitchen and bathroom, and Victor was attracted to the small study included on the ground floor and the double garage. The price of the largest plot was £6,950 so there would have to be some tightening of belts, but the idea of having a brand new house in a sought-after area was very appealing.

Victor put Cotswold Close up for sale and almost immediately had a buyer agreeing to the purchase price of £5,250. No longer was there time to consider the new build property, and the race to find another home began in earnest. A semi-detached house came up for sale on the south side Bedford in Gloucester Road, barely a mile from where Hilda worked. That seemed very convenient, because it would mean there would no longer be the need for the daily taxi or the bus. They arranged to view the property the day it was advertised in the local paper, made an offer of £5,200, and put down a deposit.

Gloucester Road (1971 - 1973)

The moving process went well until the final few days, when suddenly the seller became unresponsive and did not remove their furniture from the house immediately after exchange of contracts as had been agreed. A new date for completion was arranged between the respective solicitors, and the seller eventually made contact with an apology and confirmed that the house would be emptied a week prior to the moving in date.

On 26th July 1971, the same day that the United States launched the Apollo 15 moon mission, Victor, Hilda and Hilary moved into 6 Gloucester Road. Countdown was put on hold for an hour when a last minute hitch meant that they had to wait outside with the furniture van until it was sorted out, but apart from that the move went smoothly.

6 Gloucester Road, Bedford, 1990

Although in good decorative order, the house needed a lick of paint to freshen it up. Once they had settled in, Victor set to with his decorating materials and changed the colour of all the woodwork to magnolia.

Neither Victor nor Hilda had noticed when they viewed the house that there were very few electrical power points. Each of the ground floor rooms had one single mains outlet; there was none in the entrance lobby and hallway. Although the two double bedrooms had a single socket each, the small bedroom was lacking any means of plugging in a mains appliance, as was the landing. Clearly, there would need to be some extra power points installed.

While checking out the existing electrical installation, it was discovered that the wiring was rubber insulated and showed signs of deterioration. The house needed rewiring using modern cable, at the same time adding extra mains outlets in all the rooms.

In October, Victor and Hilda wrote a wish list for where they wanted the new sockets, with plenty in each room, and Phil drew up a detailed plan for installing new ring circuits. The ground floor had a deep space beneath the floorboards which would make running the cables an easier task than would a concrete floor, so Victor and Phil decided they could carry out the work between them. Over the duration of a week, in the daytime Victor raised floorboards where access was needed and chased channels in the wall plaster up to the socket positions, and Phil arrived each evening to install the wiring and fit the sockets.

The next big job was to tackle the kitchen. Victor fitted new cupboards at ground and wall level as well as Formica work surfaces, which were in vogue at the time. To protect the surfaces, he made a few matching cutting boards which are still in use by the family to the present day. He shelved plans to replace the old floor-standing Gloworm solid fuel boiler which provided hot water. It vented to the outdoors through a huge cast iron flue, and the disruption that would be caused to replace it with a wall-mounted modern version would have been substantial.

Triumph had upgraded the Vitesse to a 1998cc six cylinder engine in 1966, and in 1968 introduced a Mark 2 version with upgraded suspension and engine tweaks which pushed the power up even further. The car's performance was comparable to the MGB sports car, and Victor found the idea irresistible. He traded in the one purchased less than eighteen months previously for the more potent model. On 11th July 1972, he became the proud owner of a 1969 Mark 2 Triumph Vitesse, registration MBM 791G.

Although cars were on the verge of becoming less amenable to being serviced and repaired by the amateur mechanic, and the need for regularly sliding underneath with a grease gun had long passed, it was not unusual for enthusiastic owners to tackle quite complex jobs. Just a few weeks after Victor had taken delivery of the Mark 2 Vitesse, he decided to remove the cylinder head and check out the condition of the cylinders. This turned out to be quite a complex task, because the engine had six cylinders and modern overhead cams. However, the engine was partially disassembled, inspected, 'de-coked', and put back together over the course of one weekend.

In August 1972, Hilary was engaged to be married to Nigel Worker, a car bodywork specialist from Kempston. Hilary and Nigel had plans to build their own house on land given to them by Nigel's grandparents at the end of Church Walk in Kempston. As a temporary measure, they located a static mobile home on the site while drawing up plans and making arrangements for the house to be built at what would become house number 37A.

Arrangements for the wedding were under way early in 1973, and on 14th April that year Hilary and Nigel were married at St. Mary's Church in Bedford. All Hilda's family from the north east travelled down for the occasion: Florrie, Alice, Allan and Marion, nephew David, and nieces Barbara and Helen. Bridesmaids Barbara and Helen wore dresses made by Florrie from material chosen and sent up to Middlesbrough by Hilary.

Hilda (left) at Hilary and Nigel's Wedding, April 1973

A lavish reception was held after the wedding at the Transfiguration Church Hall in Kempston, well attended by friends and family. After the reception, the couple spent a night at the Park Hotel overlooking the River Great Ouse in Bedford. Although they did not realise at the time, the river was going to play a huge part in the rest of their lives together. The following day they set off for their honeymoon on the Isle of Wight.

Florrie and Alice had taken the long distance bus from Middlesbrough to Bedford, which was a tiring 200 mile journey lasting around five hours, so stayed over with Hilda and Victor for a few days before catching the bus back. Alan, Marion and Hilary's cousins had travelled down in their family's Volkswagen Beetle, and booked into a small bed and breakfast in Great Barford, just a handful of miles outside Bedford, so they did not have to return home the same day.

Leading up to Hilary's wedding, Victor and Hilda had been looking ahead and decided that the Gloucester Road house was far too big for two, although that alone would not have initiated another move. The deciding factor was that the demographics of the area had altered over a very short period, and Victor was concerned about the potential effect on the value of their house. So, even though it was less than two years since they had moved in, and the location was ideal for Hilda's work, it was time to think about selling up. The house was put on the market for £11,500 with the estate agent's description stating quite prominently that each room had two double power points! The property sold for £10,650 on 2nd April 1973, although it would be nearly three months before completion.

Pax Hill (1973 - 2010)

On 18th June 1973, Hilda and Victor exchanged contracts with the seller of 16 Pax Hill, and took possession on 12th July.

16 Pax Hill with Triumph Vitesse Mk2 in drive, 1974

Although he had no idea when they decided to purchase the house, the next door neighbour turned out to be Pete Goldsmith, an old work colleague of Victor's from E.J. Day. This turned out to be a mixed blessing, because Pete was very proud of his garden and Victor was soon to discover a problem which would affect him for the rest of his life. Hilda, though, would have a great deal to thank their neighbours for in her later years.

One of the first jobs that Victor tackled was to make some changes to the back garden. It had an open aspect, with the ability to see down its full length from the lounge. Victor recognised that the opposite was also true, and that neighbours at the bottom of their adjoining garden were able to see their lounge and kitchen windows.

So, not long after moving in, Victor erected a six foot fence across the garden about six yards from the house to give some privacy. He cleared and levelled the area between the fence and the house, putting down layers of hardcore and lime with a generous helping of chipped stone on top. At the same time, he arranged for a shed to be erected on a paved base at the end of the concrete driveway that ran from the road along the side of the house.

To Victor's dismay, the seasonal rainy weather in the autumn of 1973 showed up a problem with the garden. Water accumulated around the edge of the flower beds, eventually running towards the house and then, because of a slight slope to the concrete drive, underneath a fence into their neighbour's garden. It was not a small trickle, but a steady stream which threatened to create a serious amount of bitterness between Victor and Pete Goldsmith. Victor tried to establish whether the problem had existed before they moved in, but their neighbour was not very communicative.

Thinking that the cause might be the work he had carried out to create the cleared area at the top of the garden preventing the passage of water below the surface, Victor came up with a plan to solve the problem. He dug a channel across the width of the garden about 30 inches deep and 18 inches wide, the bottom of which sloped to a large pit in front of the garden shed which he hoped would act as a soak-away. The channel and the pit were disguised with paving slabs on top. Sadly the plan did not work, because after a day or two the channel and pit filled with water and overflowed underneath the fence as before.

Victor came up with another plan. He purchased a large submersible pump and about 50 feet of strong hose which he laid along the edge of the drive almost to the entrance at the road. Then he replaced one of the paving slabs covering the pit with a strong wooden cover which could easily be removed. Connecting the pump to the hose, he lowered it into the pit and drained the water.

The new plan worked in the sense that the neighbour no longer had water flowing into his garden, but because the pit filled up even if there had not been any significant rainfall, Victor had unknowingly initiated a nightly ritual of 'pumping out' which only ended shortly before he died almost 20 years later.

By 1976, the Vitesse was showing signs of rust underneath, and in particular the chassis 'outriggers' had started to deteriorate, a well-documented weak spot on that particular car. For some time, Victor had wanted a small van for running errands and transporting items which either would not fit into the Vitesse, or were on their way to the local rubbish dump. On 21st November 1976, Nigel sold him a 1965 Austin Mini Traveller registration LTW447C for the strangely exact amount of £156.95 which not only satisfied the need for a van but also meant that Victor had transport while the Vitesse was being repaired.

Proper Pride, which had been taken over by Kayser Bondor some years previously, was hit with difficult trading conditions in 1977, and re-organised its accounting systems. The work that was carried out in the Bedford accounts department was moved elsewhere and Hilda was given formal notice of redundancy in August 1977. She left the company after over 14 years on 9th September 1977. Although there was a redundancy payment made, Hilda decided to take a lump sum from her pension account with the company, and a reduced weekly pension. She claimed unemployment benefit until December the following year, after which she decided it was probably not worthwhile looking for another job since she would reach retirement age in August 1980.

The house was heated by a Parkray solid fuel burner, and an electric storage heater in the main bedroom. Although the solid fuel heating was just adequate, with winter approaching and Hilda at home all day, and with her redundancy payment in the bank, central heating seemed a good idea. Copper microbore pipe was a very popular choice in the 1970s, and was cheaper to buy and easier to install with less disruption than the larger conventional pipework. That seemed an ideal solution, so in the winter of 1977 Victor arranged for it to be installed together with a boiler mounted behind a modern gas fire in the living room.

Although the Triumph Vitesse was running perfectly well, and still bringing a smile to Victor's lips whenever he drove it, the rust problem with the outriggers ate into the chassis and eventually won the day. With a heavy heart, Victor part exchanged the car in 1981 for a more sedate 1973 Hillman Avenger estate. But the heavy car, coupled with a 1300cc engine, was too sluggish for Victor even though he was slowing down as he grew older. In 1975, Hillman had brought out a more lively version with a 1600cc engine and just a year after buying the first Victor traded it in for the newer model. That would be the car that was to outlive its owner.

As Hilda and Victor grew older, new life was in the making. Hilary and Nigel presented them with three grandchildren, starting with Jeff who was born on 16th June 1978. Gary followed a couple of years later on 6th January 1981, and Laura was born 11th May 1985.

Victor had never been one for staying in the same job for long, and wanted to make what was probably going to be his final move while he was still in his fifties. The Bedford County Press, owned by Westminster Press, printed a range of local newspapers, and had moved from their premises in Mill Street to a new plant on Goldington Road. Their press was the largest and most advanced in Europe at the time and they were looking for additional staff to handle their expansion. Victor made a successful application and left Sidney Press in February 1979, a few months before his 60th birthday. Had he stayed at Sidney Press a few more years, he would have been entitled to a redundancy payment as they closed down and the site was developed for housing in 1982.

One day in early March 1981, Victor arrived home from his shift at the County Press complaining of severe chest pains. The doctor was called, diagnosed a collapsed lung, and Victor was rushed to Bedford General Hospital that same day. Although he was in pain, the hospital waited to see whether the lung would re-inflate on its own, but after it became clear that was not going to happen they resorted to draining the air through the insertion of a chest tube.

It would be several days before Victor had the chest tube removed, and two more before he was able to return home. Further investigations revealed that the collapsed lung had been caused by the beginnings of emphysema almost certainly because of Victor's pipe and cigarette smoking over the years.

The scare was enough to encourage Victor to stop smoking. Although Hilda only smoked occasionally, and used menthol cigarettes such as Solent and Consulate which were thought to be a safer option, she agreed to give up at the same time to make things easier for Victor. In practice, Hilda did not completely stop smoking for a number of years, but refrained in Victor's presence.

After 18 years of being in debt to the local building society, early in 1981 the mortgage on Pax Hill was showing only £33.04 owing. Unfortunately, the letter to inform Hilda and Victor that the final payment would mean they could claim the house deeds held by the building society arrived just as Victor was admitted to hospital with his collapsed lung. Hilda called in and made the usual payment, but was too distracted by Victor's condition to realise the significance of what she had done. After he recovered and returned home, on 7th April 1981 the couple visited the Gateway Building Society and took possession of the deeds to the house.

The work Victor was carrying out at County Press had become less demanding as the years passed, because of the adoption of computerised systems for preparing copy, proof reading and type setting. Also, the public were becoming more tolerant of minor mistakes in magazines and newspapers so in many ways the job of a proof reader had become less onerous. Victor managed to continue working as a reader with County Press until his retirement in August 1984 on his 65th birthday.

Victor's emphysema grew worse after retirement, and by the end of the 1980s he was struggling to breathe comfortably. Oxygen had no effect, and inhalers to open his airways did little to help. Driving his car became difficult, and he was forced to stop what had been regular visits to Stevenage for a meal at Christine and Phil's house.

By 1992, he could no longer climb the stairs unaided and had to be helped up by Hilda pulling on a d-i-y harness he fashioned out of old trouser belts.

The doctor was called on many occasions, but Hilda was told there was nothing that could be done. By the summer of 1993, Victor took to his bed and refused to get up. He would not receive visitors, and began to talk incessantly, mostly gibberish.

Victor died on 11th November 1993, Armistice Day, at around eleven o'clock in the morning. A quiet family funeral was held at Fosterhill Road cemetery in Bedford on 19th November at 1130, and Victor's ashes were scattered in the Garden of Remembrance.

Following Victor's death, Hilda began to look to the future with a new energy. The first major change she made was to have double glazed windows installed. Although Victor had painstakingly looked after the wooden frames as best he could, the work had become too difficult for him to manage in later life. The front entrance had been problematic ever since they had moved into the property over twenty years earlier, with water seeping through cracks in the concrete facing above the door. A replacement door and window unit solved that problem, and at the same time made the hall warmer and smartened up the front of the house.

The driveway was looking tired, so Hilda arranged for it to be skimmed with a layer of tarmac and then painted. Also in poor condition was the wooden fence which separated Hilda's drive with the neighbour's so that was removed. The plan was to replace it, but the drives were at slightly different levels and that provided enough indication of the boundary, so the idea was abandoned.

The land boundary on the attached house next door was not so simple to sort out though. Hilda received notification of a planning application to extend the rear of their property, which entailed removing the garden fence and building along the boundary line. Hilary took Hilda to the council offices to examine the plans and everything appeared to be in order. The only concern was that the height of the extension would reduce the amount of light to the living room window, but on the other hand it would also afford a degree of privacy from next door. The work went ahead, but the extension wall appeared to encroach on to Hilda's boundary line to the extent that the fence between the two properties did not align with the wall. Hilda decided not to pursue a complaint, but the gap in the fence was never resolved.

Hilda needed someone to look after the large garden. The front was not too difficult to keep tidy, just the grass to mow and a small flower bed around the edge to weed occasionally. There was more grass in the back garden though, and a large number of rose bushes which had grown to quite a height and girth, as well as an assortment of ornamental bushes, a substantial laurel hedge, and conifers.

Phil tried to keep on top of the garden for a while during evening visits, but eventually a regular gardener was arranged by Age Concern. The hourly rate was quite high though, and there were a few instances of the gardener not turning up as promised, so the arrangement was cancelled.

Nigel knew just the person to help. Peter Frossell was not only a local well-respected landscape gardener, he was also a frequent customer at Bedford Autopanels. Peter was only too happy to take on some new business even though it was only a couple of hours every few weeks. Such is the world of coincidence, what Nigel didn't know was that Peter Frossell was Phil's cousin. Peter grew up on Wick End Farm in Stagsden, and Phil spent some happy times staying on the farm with his uncle and aunt playing on the tractors, watching the milking and eating home-made bread and jam.

By the end of the 1990s, the outside of the house had been transformed and looked very well kept. There was just one job left to be tackled. It had been many years since Victor had been able to climb a ladder to paint the old iron gutters and bargeboards, and this was the next job on Hilda's list. The bargeboards were replaced with white pvc, together with the gutters and downpipes.

Turning 80 years old in August 2000, Hilda's mobility was beginning to wane. The bathroom and toilet was downstairs which was not the most convenient arrangement for night-time use, so she and Hilary came up with a plan to convert the small third bedroom to a shower room and toilet.

Because the bedroom had been used as a store for Victor's tools and bits and pieces, they decided to partition it into two sections, one small area which could be shelved and used to keep anything useful and the bulk of the bedroom to be converted to a shower room. There was enough space to fit a shower, toilet and wash basin together with a small central heating radiator. The only major problem was connecting into the existing soil pipe, but this was overcome by fitting a new one to the outside wall and running it underground to the nearby pipe from the downstairs bathroom.

A reasonable quotation from a local plumber was agreed, and the work went without a hitch. The only problem was fitting a whole bedroom's worth of tools and miscellaneous hardware into the reduced storage area. Somehow, with a large number of deep shelves, it all fitted in.

In 2002, Hilda's eyesight began to cause problems. She loved to do the crossword each day, but it was becoming harder to read the newspaper, and watching the television was also difficult. The optician diagnosed cataracts in both eyes, and made a hospital referral for them to be treated. There was only a short wait before Hilda had the first eye remedied, then a couple of months later she had the other one operated upon. Both operations worked perfectly and she had no more trouble with her vision for the rest of her life.

For Hilda's 85th birthday, Hilary and Nigel arranged for a surprise family celebration at one of their favourite Indian restaurants in Kempston, the Blue Ginger. Hilda was not expecting the whole family to be there when she arrived, and the evening turned out to be very enjoyable. As she was not one for spicy food, the management arranged for something mild on the menu although there was considerable competition amongst the men as to who would order the hottest curry.

Hilda and family on her 85th birthday at Blue Ginger, Kempston, August 2005

It was to be a busy time socially for Hilda, because on 17th September 2005, six weeks after her birthday, her grandson Gary and Denise were married at the ancient 13th century St. Mary's Church in Denise's home village of Wootton.

Hilary had taken Hilda to buy a new outfit for the wedding, and she was in good spirits when she arrived at the church with Christine and Phil. The congregation was filmed as they walked from the road to the church entrance and Hilda gave a big smile to the camera.

Everything went to plan during the ceremony, including tears of joy from Denise as she arrived at Gary's side. The vicar knew he had a captive audience and took a while with the introductions, readings and getting to the blessing. A sigh of relief rippled through the congregation when it was time for the register to be signed.

After the official photographs had been taken in the grounds behind the church, Gary and Denise made their way to The Embankment on the Great Ouse in Bedford. More photographs were taken in the less formal setting, with the river and bridges as the backdrop.

Hilda at Gary and Denise's wedding, September 2005

The reception was held at Biddenham Pavilion, with the main hall set out in a traditional manner with tables for groups of six and a top table for the bride and groom and close family. The toasts and speeches were very entertaining and the meal enjoyable, with copious bottles of Rioja brought over from Spain by Denise's parents.

Hilda's physical health became more of a worry as each month passed, and in April 2006 a Carelink device was installed which would alert the family should there be an emergency. In theory, this was a very good idea, because all Hilda had to do was press a button on a transmitter on a lanyard worn around her neck should she get into difficulties. If nobody answered, the system called an emergency warden who would immediately attend the house to see what the problem was. However, Hilda was far less concerned about her situation, rarely remembered to wear the transmitter, and did not fully understand how it worked.

Just one year after Gary and Denise's wedding, Hilda's other grandson Jeff and Melanie arranged to get married at St. Andrew's Church on Kimbolton Road in Bedford. There was a lot for Hilary and Nigel to take care of, so Christine and Phil arranged to pick Hilda up and take her to the church. When they arrived at Pax Hill, Hilda was ready to leave but decided at the last minute that she ought to change what she was wearing. It was not until Hilary saw her at the church that anyone noticed she had changed into the same dress as she had worn for Gary's wedding and left her new outfit at home on the bed.

There was considerable excitement waiting for the bride and her father to arrive at the church, because they were arriving by a carriage pulled by a pair of handsome dapple grey horses. Although it is well known that the bride is allowed to be a little late arriving, the wedding was already running 25 minutes behind time when the carriage and pair set off to pick up the bride, and the vicar was getting quite exasperated. She was quite short with those of us still outside the church taking photographs of the horses, and suggested in no uncertain terms that we should take our seats!

The wedding ceremony went without a hitch, and Hilda gave a chuckle when Jeff was kneeling for the first blessing and it was pointed out to her that he had 'Help' written on the sole of one shoe and 'Me!' written on the other.

Hilda at Jeff and Mel's wedding, September 2006

The carriage and pair returned after the wedding, and Hilda watched as Jeff and Melanie sped away towards the Park Inn on the bank of the Great Ouse for the wedding reception.

A formal affair, based upon the pageantry surrounding wedding breakfasts in times gone by, the wedding reception was led by a Master of Ceremonies. Jeff had seated Hilda on the same table as Christine, Phil, Gary and Denise so she had people around her she knew and trusted. The line of people who had welcomed everyone as they entered the reception hall disappeared, only to file back in to be seated at the top table to the accompaniment of a slow hand clap organised by the MC. The speeches and toasts were well delivered, with instructions that the men should be 'Jackets on' or 'Jackets off' at the appropriate times.

Once the ceremonial reception was over, the top table marched out of the hall to another slow hand clap. Family and close friends made their way to the open bar area for informal drinks, where the bride and groom joined the party in full wedding attire. It wasn't long before Hilda looked at her watch and declared that she wanted to leave; it had been a long day for someone 86 years of age.

Sadly, Jeff and Melanie's wedding was to be the last social occasion when Hilda would join in with the rest of her family all together in one place. She would have been sad to know that she would not attend her granddaughter Laura's wedding, which would take place in another ten years.

Laura met her husband-to-be Scott at work, where they were employed in the same department. They began a serious relationship and moved in together, and on 26th July 2014 Laura gave birth to their first child, Alyssa.

A wedding was planned for three years hence, when Alyssa would be old enough to take part and enjoy the occasion. The couple were married on 23rd August 2017 at Bassmead Manor Barns, a stunning wedding venue tucked away inside a medieval moat in the beautiful Cambridgeshire countryside not far from St. Neots.

The ceremony took place in a 300 year old beamed barn steeped in history, after which the guests enjoyed fine catering, speeches and refreshments, and an evening of entertainment and dancing.

Laura and Scott's wedding

The following summer, on 13th June 2018, Riley was born. Neither he nor Alyssa had the pleasure of meeting their great grandmother.

Another year on, Hilda was beginning to show some signs of forgetfulness and mild confusion so in July 2007, Hilary and Phil discussed the need to set up a power of attorney over Hilda's financial and health affairs. The application forms were completed, and Phil made certain that Hilda knew exactly what powers they would have and how they could be used before she signed the forms. The hope was that it would never be necessary to invoke the powers, but it was a relief to know that the possibility was there should things take a turn for the worse.

By January 2008, Hilda had become very forgetful, would lose items around the house, had difficulty handling money and stopped wanting to go out for her usual shopping trips. A letter to Hilda's doctor, Dr. Collins, explained that mentally she was getting worse and that the family wanted to make an urgent appointment. This was set for 19th February and was attended by Hilary, Christine, Nigel and Phil who expressed their concern that Hilda needed treatment sooner rather than later. Dr. Collins made a follow up appointment for Hilda, accompanied by Hilary, and after carrying out some basic tests diagnosed that she was suffering from dementure.

Through the spring and into the summer months, Hilda's dementure worsened to the point where she asked the same questions over and over, forgot names, recent events or what was said just minutes previously and was unable to hold a coherent conversation. She became unsteady on her feet and started to suffer dizzy spells.

Another visit to Dr. Collins resulted in a battery of memory and neuropsychological tests at Bedford Hospital and an occupational therapy assessment at home. She was diagnosed with late onset Alzheimer's disease, but was not considered a suitable candidate for the drug Aricept which was known to delay further deterioration.

There was nothing that could be done, so Hilda struggled on with daily visits from Hilary, and from Christine and Phil three evenings each week. Hilary arranged for a hot meal to be delivered at lunchtime by Apetito, but Hilda did not always answer the door and even if she did, she would sometimes forget to eat the meal.

Early in January 2008, about two o'clock in the night, Hilary had a phone call from Hilda's neighbour, Pete Goldsmith. Hilda had knocked on their door and clearly thought she was home. She had a letter in her hand, and said she couldn't find the post box.

January was a bad month weather-wise, with winter storms raging across the south of England bringing heavy rain and snow. Night temperatures fell to well below freezing point, schools were closed, and the icy conditions caused many casualties on roads and exposed areas.

Hilary drove to Pax Hill to collect Hilda, and made sure she was safely in bed before leaving. To prevent that happening again, it was decided to change the front door locking system for one that needed a key before it could be opened. Unfortunately the existing door could not be modified, so the whole door and frame was replaced. There was a vanishingly small chance that Hilda would be trapped inside in the event of an emergency, but that was far less likely than the inherent danger of her taking herself for another walk in the middle of the night. She could still open the back door into the garden if she had to get out of the house quickly, but the garden gates were locked to keep her safe.

Even though Hilda's dementure was getting worse, there was always time for a celebration.

Hilda 88, with Christine, Hilary, and Grand-daughter Laura

In August 2008, a small get-together took place at Stevenage to mark her 88th birthday. Hilda appeared to enjoy the occasion which had three generations together at the same time, and made short work of her chocolate cake.

Towards the end of 2008, another plea was made to have Hilda prescribed Aricept but although Dr. Collins appeared receptive to the idea, the experts at Bedford Hospital still felt that it would not help. The drug was regularly used to treat confusion in Alzheimer's disease, improving memory, awareness and the ability to comprehend what is happening. However, there seemed to be some uncertainty over side effects and long term issues so perhaps that was why it was not considered suitable.

The family rallied around to try to make life as normal and easy for Hilda as they could, and this included the Christmas festivities at Hilary's house in Kempston. The photograph below shows Hilda with an electronic picture frame, loaded with a slideshow of old family snaps. The hope was that she would recognise them, and that by having it on when she was at home it would help bring back some memories.

Hilda with Laura, Hilary and Christine, Christmas 2008

Recent years had been busy in terms of babies, and between 2007 and 2009 Hilda had become a great grandmother three times over. In March 2007, Gary and Denise presented her with great grandson Steven and in December that year, Jeff and Melanie had great granddaughter Chloe. Then in February 2009, Gary and Denise had their second child Lewis, a third great grandson for Hilda.

Although it was known that Hilda had always been generous when it came to supporting charities, the full extent of her donations was not apparent until after her diagnosis with Alzheimer's. For years, she had been writing cheques, some of them for large amounts, to her favourite charities. As her mental state worsened, she began to reply with a cheque to every request that dropped through the letterbox.

By January 2009, three or four charity letters were arriving each day, and some charities were clearly writing again as soon as they received a donation. Hilda did not remember writing any cheques, and it was worrying that there was an occasional blank stub in the chequebook.

Phil started a campaign to stop the letters, and wrote to each charity every time they sent an appeal for money. Some replied with an acknowledgement, but most ignored the requests, and six months on the letters were still arriving although at a vastly reduced rate. Clearly Hilda had made a strong impression and further pleas were not going to make much difference, but eventually they dwindled to the point where they could be ignored.

The year 2010 began badly, with Hilda becoming more withdrawn and unable to carry out day to day activities; it was time to get in some professional help. Dr. Collins had left the local surgery, but his replacement was happy to give a referral for daily assistance.

By March, a carer from the Alzheimer's Society was visiting each morning to make sure Hilda was up and dressed and had eaten some breakfast and had a drink. The drink check was vital, because she had been through periods of forgetting to take any fluids and that added to her state of confusion. Hilary would visit early in the afternoon to ensure Hilda had eaten her meal from Apetito, and a carer would follow later.

The time had clearly arrived when Hilda was no longer able to take responsibility for her affairs and on 12th April 2010 Phil and Hilary applied to the Office of the Public Guardian to register the Power of Attorney that Hilda had signed in 2007. All close family members were informed, including Hilda's brother Allan. Sadly though, Allan was also suffering from dementure by this time and had been living in a care home since February 2010. This was a major step to take, but Hilda's health was never going to improve and it was recognised that some significant dilemmas were waiting around the corner. The Power of Attorney registration was completed in June. By July, the carer visits were increased to three each day.

On 13th August, Hilda's ninetieth birthday, Hilary was away on holiday but travelled back to celebrate the occasion. The special day was marked by a special birthday cake arranged by Christine's local bakery.

Hilda's 90th Birthday, at home with Christine and Hilary

Hilda's birthday was a turning point when the family recognised that she would not be able to continue living alone for much longer. She began to stay in bed longer in the mornings, and not get up for when the carer called. Quite often, the door would go unanswered when her midday meal was delivered. By September, an arrangement had to be put into place for the Apetito driver to leave the meal in a container by the front door if there was no answer, and call a member of the family, who would then ring Hilda to go and retrieve it.

On the morning of 16th November, the Alzheimer's carer could not get a reply to the doorbell, so let herself in with the key from the outside key-safe. Hilda was lying at the bottom of the stairs, and was thought to have been there for some hours. An ambulance was called, and Hilda was taken to Bedford General. Although she was not seriously injured, the fall had shaken her confidence and she would spend the best part of a month in hospital.

Marston Moretaine (2010 - 2012)

Full time care was going to be needed once Hilda was able to leave hospital, and a meeting was arranged with Social Services for 12th December. The risks were clear: falling over, personal neglect, dehydration, vulnerability to attack, robbery and fraud were all considered high risks. The possibility of medicine overdose, locking herself in or out, and not understanding how to call for help were some of the medium level risks discussed. All of those things had actually occurred previously so they presented a real cause for concern.

The social workers agreed that regular visits from carers in her own home would no longer keep Hilda safe. Hilary had already collected information on care homes in and around Bedford, and the family had been discussing the various options since Hilda's fall. Grandson Jeffery's mother in law was a professional care worker, and out of the four possibilities she recommended The Old Village School Nursing Home in Marston Moretaine.

Old Village School Nursing Home at Marston Morteyne, near Bedford

Fortunately, the nursing home had a vacancy, so arrangements could quickly go ahead. Hilda was able to move in on 18th December 2010. The council agreed to pay for the first twelve weeks of care, although this needed to be topped up because the weekly rate was higher than the council's standard allowance. That period gave the family some breathing space to get Hilda's finances in good order. The possibility of the Primary Care Trust continuing to pay the fees was investigated under their scheme for handling the need for continuing health care, but their representative deemed that Hilda was not eligible and would have to self-fund the cost of her accommodation and nursing care.

Hilda soon settled into the daily routine at the nursing home, and didn't appear to miss her home at Pax Hill. The carers were friendly, and Hilda's room was clean and light, with a window looking out into one of the gardens. There were no restrictions on visiting, and Hilda soon had a stock of biscuits, tea and coffee which the family could use to make drinks in the communal kitchen. There were some teething problems, mostly caused by the staff's lack of experience looking after Alzheimer's patients, but these were ironed out over time. Hilary would visit most days, and Phil would drive Christine over from Stevenage on three evenings each week.

By the summer of 2011, it was obvious that Hilda would never return to Pax Hill and in July her house was put up for sale. Leaving it standing empty would bring the risk of vandalism or possibly squatters. Bills for insurance, council tax and utilities were still having to be paid, and the weekly fees from the nursing home were seriously depleting Hilda's savings. A prospective buyer made an offer on the house of around 5% less than the asking price and this was accepted. The house sale went through without any major hitches, and was completed in October.

Hilda started to leave her room very occasionally, making her way to the communal hall where patients could sit and chat, watch a massive television or eat their meals. She had visits from the family on her 91st birthday on 13th August, and the walls of her room were decorated with greetings cards and banners. The rest of the year slipped past with no major incidents.

Hilda, with Christine and Phil, at The Old Village School Nursing Home, Christmas 2011

Christmas had been a happy occasion for Hilda, but shortly afterwards her health took a downward turn. She was admitted to Bedford General Hospital on 27th March 2012, and spent two nights on Shuttleworth Ward. She tested positive for *clostridium difficile* and was moved from the general ward to a private room on Harpur Ward where she could be monitored closely. The prognosis seemed good, although it would be about three weeks before Hilda would be able to return to the nursing home. An X-ray taken of her stomach on 6th April didn't show up any problems other than continuing infection, but it was almost five weeks later, on 1st May, that Hilda had improved sufficiently to return to the Old Village School.

Hilda was clearly still very unwell through the month of May and in early June was either unwilling or unable to eat or drink. She gave no sign of recognising anyone who visited and was confined to her bed most of the time. Hilary and Nigel had been sitting with her on 10th June, but the care home staff said they should take a break and go home for a meal and a rest. Sadly, Hilda died while they were gone.

Hilda's funeral was held in Bedford at Norse Road crematorium on 25th June, 2012 attended by her close family.

Hilda's funeral flowers

On 3rd August, 2012, which would have been her 92nd birthday, Hilda's ashes were scattered in front of the memorial stone where those of her parents James and Florence Gott had been strewn some 65 years previously at their favourite holiday retreat in Glaisdale.

Siblings Florrie, Alice and Allan

Florence Emily Gott (1909 - 1977)

Florence, known to the family as Florrie, was born 4th November 1909 at 3 Benson Street, Linthorpe, Middlesbrough. She was the first of three girls and a boy to be born to Florence and James Gott over a period of 13 years, although sadly their next child would survive for only a month. Florrie was baptised by William Barrett, the curate at St. Barnabas Church, on 24th November.

Although she briefly had a younger sister at the age of four, Florrie would be six years old and have started school before the next child was born a year after the beginning of the Great War. Life was hard, and It would not have been long before Florrie was helping to look after her little sister. By the time the next two children had arrived she was 13 years old and expected to help out with the family duties. One year later Florrie left school, and a year after that she gained a brother. This meant that at the age of 15 she was kept busy lending a hand to her mother, looking after her younger siblings.

The slump of the 1920s hit the north east of England hard, and fitting in her household responsibilities with paid work was difficult. Florrie had a natural talent for sewing, and although she could have found a position in one of the many clothing factories in the area she took on small dressmaking jobs at home.

Still living at 3 Benson Street at the start of the Second World War in 1939, Florrie was working from home as a dressmaker. She was not called up for war service, as she was over 30 years old when war broke out and enlistment was only required for women between the ages of 20 and 30. Her sewing continued though, and she began to specialise in making wedding dresses.

Florrie married Isaac Dobson Austin from Hull, five years her senior, in the late summer of 1940 at Middlesbrough Register Office. Prior to the marriage, Isaac was working as a labourer and living with his mother Sarah at 33 Kingston Street, Middlesbrough. Kingston Street is about the same distance north of Albert Park as Benson Street is to the south and less than a mile as the crow flies.

Florrie and Isaac's wedding with Hilda and Isaac's brother Alfred

The marriage to Ike was only to last a few years. He and Florrie were amicably divorced in the 1940s and Florrie moved in with her sister Alice at 42 Eastborne Road, Middlesbrough. Ike did not marry again. He died on 7th July 1977 at the age of 74, and was buried at Linthorpe Cemetery four days later.

Florrie's father James Gott had been employed by Middlesbrough Corporation since he and Florence married, and steadily worked his way up from gardener to deputy park superintendant at Albert Park. Albert Park is only a short walk from Benson Street and the family will have known it well. All the children spent hours in the park as they grew up, and is most likely where Florrie set eyes upon, or more likely heard shouting in the distance 'All park skates!', John Robert Ellis.

John Robert Ellis, or Bob as he was known to the family, was born in Thornaby-on-Tees on 5th February 1905. As a small child he lived at 9 Clarendon Road, Middlesbrough where his parents Matthew James and Mary Elizabeth lodged with their uncle, George Howe. George was a Horse Driver for Middlesbrough Corporation, and Bob's father worked as a casting contractor at the local steel works. George's cousin Frederick, a joiner in the house building industry, also lived in the same house.

Bob married 18 year old Lily Gibson, from Batley, in July 1924 and they had two children, Freda and Raymond. He and Lily lived at 24 Beechgrove Road, Middlesbrough. The marriage fizzled out after the children left home, the couple divorced, and Bob returned to live with his parents who had bought a house at 4 Arlington Road, Middlesbrough.

For many years, Bob worked as a gardener at Albert Park, just like Florrie's father James. Since he was working on the land this probably exempted him from war service during WW2. The park's history goes back to 1864, when the town's mayor Henry Bolckow bought some land off Linthorpe Road and gave it to Middlesbrough Borough Council for use as a public amenity. It was officially opened in 1868 and named after Prince Albert.

A roller skating rink was established in the south east quarter of the park behind the lakeside pavilion in 1947, screened by hedges and surrounded by terraced seating areas.

Although Bob enjoyed his gardening activities, he preferred to help out at the new rink and took on the role of roller skate mechanic, looking after the skates and repairing faults to keep them in good condition. After a while he ran the rink more or less single handed, playing the music, taking the entrance money and handing the skates out to visitors. Then, at the end of each session, he would shout 'All park skates! All park skates!'

Albert Park skating rink and Bob on duty

Whether it was a chance meeting, or Florrie had purposely sought out Bob after seeing him at the skating rink, or even maybe because her father and Bob were work colleagues and there was some kind of collaboration going on, Florrie and Bob became more than good friends. They married on Saturday 30th June 1951 at Middlesbrough Register Office. Witnesses at the wedding were Florrie's sister Alice and her husband John Lawrence Gale.

After they were married, Florrie and Bob moved in with his parents at 4 Arlington Road. Bob's father Matthew suffered badly from rheumatoid arthritis and died at home of senile myocarditis aged 78 on 24th July 1958. Florrie registered his death the following day. Bob's mother, Mary, had heart problems and after contracting bronchitis and pneumonia she died from acute congestive cardiac failure at home on 22nd April 1963.

Florrie and Bob's wedding, family group, 1951

Bob developed a corneal ulcer in his right eye in the mid 1960s which would not respond to treatment. It could have been caused by an infection, but also by chemical or physical trauma. Although he went through extensive treatments, nothing worked so the only solution was to stitch his eyelid closed. That is how he is remembered by most of the surviving family.

Florrie and Bob lived happily at Arlington Road with their small poodle Fifi. Florrie continued making wedding dresses as she had done through the years, and her front room was frequently filled with them in various stages of manufacture. In April 1973, Florrie made the bridesmaid dresses which her nieces Barbara and Helen would wear at Hilda's daughter Hilary's wedding.

In 1977 Florrie endured a few months of what she thought was heartburn. The truth, though, was much worse and her heart was the underlying cause of her discomfort.. After suffering a full-blown heart attack, Florrie was rushed to hospital but there was little they could do. She died on 26th August 1977.

Bob contracted rectum cancer in his seventies, and in 1981 was admitted to Hemlington Hospital in Middlesbrough where he died on 31st May after the cancer had spread across his body.

Florrie, Bob and Fifi at Arlington Road, 1969

Lily Gott (1913-1913)

James and Florence's second child, Lily, died shortly after birth. She was born on 10th July 1913 at home in Benson Street, but contracted pneumonia after three weeks.

Caused by bacteria or a virus, pneumonia can be very dangerous for babies because their immune system is not fully developed. It kills more children globally than any other disease, claiming the lives of 800,000 in 2018. Hospitals in England recorded 56,000 emergency admissions for the disease in 2019, but deaths here are rare these days because it can be treated with antibiotics and oxygen if caught quickly enough.

Lily did not have the advantage of modern treatment for the disease, and died at home on 9th August when she was just one month old.

An inquest was held on 11th August by the Middlesbrough Coroner Oswald H Cochrane, and the cause of death was established as syncope, a reduction in blood supply to the brain, resulting from acute pneumonia.

Alice Gott (1915 - 1980)

Alice was born on 24th April 1915, nine months into the Great War. She was named after her mother's youngest sister, Aunt Alice. Although there were two brothers born after Aunt Alice, neither were to survive past childhood. Walter, born January 1898 died at the age of six and Horace, born 1900 would only live to see his second birthday.

Alice and Allan c1930

Making her way through the Linthorpe infants and junior schools, Alice progressed well. She was unsure of what career she would follow, and after leaving school in 1929 worked as a shop assistant in the local area.

At the outbreak of WW2 Alice was employed by Mantles, a well-respected dress retailer at the Stoke Emporium, later to become the Cooperative Society, on Linthorpe Road. Conscription of single women did not start until December 1941, and the requirement for married women to take on war-related work came much later.

When she had turned 25 years old, Alice married John Lawrence Gale, known to all as Lawrence. The ceremony took place on 30th November 1940 at St. Barnabas Church just around the corner from Benson Street. Hilda, who had just turned 20 years of age, was a witness to the marriage.

Alice and Lawrence Gale

Lawrence's father, John Taylor Gale, was an overseer with the General Post Office, working with telephones. He contracted sub-acute meningitis and cerebral softening and died aged 35 on 6th September 1917. John's brother Edmund Gale was with him when he died at home, at 36 Breckon Hill Road, Middlesbrough. Edmond registered the death later that same day. John left his estate to his wife Florence, who decided to move away from the old terraced house to a more modern property at 42 Eastbourne Road.

Lawrence and his sister Florence Margaret, known as Peggy, grew up at Eastbourne Road which is less than half a mile from Benson Street where Alice Gott lived. Lawrence was a gardener by trade, and might well have worked at Albert Park where he probably met Alice.

42 Eastbourne Road, Middlesbrough

Alice and Lawrence moved in with his mother and sister Peggy after they were married. There was plenty of space with a large lounge, dining room, breakfast room and kitchen downstairs, and three bedrooms and bathroom upstairs. Peggy married six months after Lawrence and moved out in the spring of 1941, and on 4th November 1944 Florence passed away which left Alice and Lawrence with the house to themselves. They were to live there until their death around half a century later.

Alice (centre) with Lawrence and his sister Peggy

Lawrence was an avid fisherman, and was equally keen on sea fishing and inland angling. He would go after flatfish and bass from the local shore or maybe from the beach at Redcar or Saltburn, or fish from one of the local piers at South Gare or Middleton where he might find mackerel, whiting and flounders. Lawrence would often set off for whole days with his long-time friend John Hutchison who lived nearby at 81 Emerson Avenue.

Around the spring of 1980, Alice went to the doctor with what was diagnosed as recurring cystitis. The usual treatments did not seem to be working, and after further investigation she was found to have advanced bladder cancer. Alice was admitted to North Ormesby Hospital in Middlesbrough, and died on 8th August 1980. Hilda and Victor travelled from Bedford to Middlesbrough for the funeral and stayed a few days with Lawrence.

John Hutchison paid Lawrence a visit on 29th August, 1991 but could not get a response when he knocked the door. Help was called for, and Lawrence was found dead on the toilet. A post-mortem discovered the cause of death to be haemopericardium due to ruptured myocardial infarction - a massive heart attack which, even if medical help had been instantly available, was unsurvivable. Lawrence's death was registered by his brother-in-law, James Wood Mason, the following day.

Lawrence owned a large plot of land at the rear of 24 Eastbourne Road, HM Land Registry title CE23298. Most of the plots behind the houses were small allotments, but as Lawrence worked for the council as head gardener at Albert Park he was probably able to buy a larger plot and his was about 104 feet long and 26 feet wide (31 x 8 metres). In recognition of their friendship, he left the land to J Huchison in his will.

Alice and Lawrence c1960

James Allan Gott (1922 - 2016)

James Allan, named after his father but known as Allan, was born at 3 Benson Street on 28th July 1922. The youngest of the four children, his eldest sister Florrie was thirteen years his senior, Alice was seven years older and Hilda was closest having been born just two years earlier.

Allan with Hilda and his parents

When Allan started school, his sister Florrie was 19 and Alice 14, so it is unsurprising that he spent much of his free time with Hilda who was much closer to his age.

Just as his sisters had done, Allan attended Linthorpe infants and junior schools on Roman Road, before moving on to Middlesbrough Junior Technical School. He left the Technical School in 1936 and began an apprenticeship with C. Horne & Co. Ltd., an electrical engineering company on Dock Street and East Street a quarter mile or so from the Transporter Bridge. Hornes made and repaired electric motors and control panels for a wide range of industrial applications. The proprietor, Charlie Horne, also owned North Eastern Refrigeration which occupied part of the same building, so the apprentices would spend time on a variety of equipments.

The apprenticeship lasted four years, with the outbreak of the Second World War taking place in his final year. Allan completed his training at about the time the Battle of Britain had been won and joined the Royal Navy towards the end of 1940. After spending his entire life sleeping on a downstairs sofa in his parents' two up two down at Benson Street, Allan joked that his hammock marked the first time he had somewhere to sleep that he could call his own!

Allan's first port of call was HMS Collingwood in Fareham, Hampshire. This was a 'concrete ship' and one of the main training establishments for new recruits. The grounds covered around 200 acres, and about 1000 trainees joined every three weeks for a ten week course. At the end of the course he would have been evaluated for his first active posting or possibly more specific training, and since he had already completed an engineering apprenticeship that would have influenced the decision.

The Royal Institute for the Blind under the name of St. Dunston's offered visually impaired servicemen holidays, convalescence, re-training perhaps as telephonists, masseurs or stenographers, and rehabilitation across many locations. One of these was at Ovingdean, near Brighton and Hove. During WW2 there was significant bombing along the south coast of England, and it was considered too dangerous for St. Dunstan's to continue to operate at Ovingdean. The residents were evacuated to other locations, and in 1940 the War Office took over the buildings. Towards the end of the war, Allan was posted to Overdean which had become the main instructional site for the Royal Navy Wireless Telegraphy Training School. The buildings were returned for use by St. Dunstan's in 1946.

Allan, Royal Navy Petty Officer, c1946

Allan had one final posting in the Royal Navy to HMS Cawsand Bay. In 1946 he sent Hilda this photograph of the vessel on which he served, in a small folder. She kept it safe her entire life.

HMS Cawsand Bay

HMS Cawsand Bay was a Bay-class frigate deployed in the Clyde area in December 1946 and soon afterwards nominated for reduction to Reserve status. She sailed to Rosyth on 11th February 1946 to join a flotilla for local duties, and sustained damage there in a collision. In March she sailed to Portsmouth, arriving on the 6th and in April was accepted into the Reserve Fleet at Portsmouth where she remained until 1958. She was sold for demolition to an Italian ship breaker and towed to Genoa to arrive 5th September 1959.

After being demobilised, Allan began a promising career with Imperial Chemical Industries (ICI). He worked at Wilton as an electrician, and for many years as electrical supervisor at the Engineering Works Services Department.

ICI started construction of a new chemical complex at Wilton in 1946, and officially opened it in 1949. Nestled between Middlesbrough and Redcar, the new facility included the manufacture of nylon, polyester, and ingredients needed for household products such as antifreeze and detergents. Such was the size of the plant, the site had its own power station providing electricity and steam for use in the manufacturing processes.

Around the same time as starting at ICI, Allan met Marion Ann Longhorn. Marion lived in Collinson Avenue in Whinney Banks, a new housing development to the south west of Linthorpe and about a mile from Benson Street. In Park Road South, opposite the south eastern corner of Albert Park, stood the local fire station, a popular venue for parties and dances. Fate came into play, and Marion and Allan found themselves in the same place at the same time. Like Hilda, though, Allan was rather shy despite his time in the Royal Navy and it was down to Marion to take the initiative in the Ladies' Excuse Me dance.

That tap on the shoulder was the start of a happy relationship which would last over sixty years. The couple married on 26th May 1951 at St. Barnabas Church in Linthorpe.

Allan and Marion's wedding 1951

Allan and Marion bought their first home at 34 Ravenscroft Avenue in Linthorpe before they married, and Marion was living there at the time of their wedding. The house was a couple of streets north of Arlington Road where Allan's sister Florrie would be living after marrying Robert Ellis the following month, and about a quarter of a mile south of Eastbourne Road where his sister Alice had lived since 1940.

34 Ravenscroft Avenue, Linthorpe (present day)

After leaving Whinney Banks School, Marion had dreams of university or becoming a teacher, but although she would have easily attained entrance qualifications the family could not afford for her to continue her education. Instead, she went to Kirkby College taking a secretarial course, which included learning shorthand. She worked at ICI Billingham and then at a solicitors' office in Middlesbrough. Marion gave up paid work after she and Allan married.

Although the house at Ravenscroft Avenue was recently built in the 1930s, it needed some attention. The couple completely renovated the property. Allan installed central heating, and replaced the rubber electrical wiring with modern cable, fitting new mains outlets at the same time. Even though they had made their home modern and comfortable, their dream was to own a smallholding. Allan loved his garden, and grew vegetables on an allotment half a mile away on Saltersgill Road.

Allan, Marion and David with sister Hilda and nieces Christine and Hilary, c1956

Allan and Marion's children were all born while they were living at Ravenscroft Avenue. David in 1955, Barbara in 1959, and Helen in 1965. Both David and Helen followed in their parents' footsteps and had jobs at ICI; Barbara went into teaching. For a short time while Helen was at secondary school, Marion worked as a dinner lady and lunchtime supervisor. Allan joked that she worked two hours each day with an hour for lunch!

Allan took early retirement from ICI in 1981 at the age of 59. His 30 years with the company earned him not only countless memories, but also a gold watch and carriage clock. His retirement was an opportunity to re-assess their life plans, and in 1983 the couple moved to Glaisdale, a pretty village in the Esk Valley countryside in the heart of the North Yorkshire Moors.

Their bungalow, which they named 'Ravenscroft', was in a beautiful location with open moorland a hundred yards in one direction and the village about the same distance in the other. The other side of the High Street, the River Esk flowed quietly through dense woodland kissing the edge of the village.

'Ravenscroft', Glaisdale, c1986

The Gott family had spent many holidays at Glaisdale and nearby Egton Bridge when Florrie, Alice, Hilda and Allan were children. Allan was in his element with the quiet and mostly deserted countryside, recollecting his childhood memories of the area. He was happy to tend the large garden, take long walks over the moors and live a solitary life. Marion, on the other hand, was a very sociable person. She joined every society and club she could think of, and delivered 'Meals on Wheels'.

Six years flashed by, and as each one passed Marion longed for more social contact and to be closer to the family. In 1989, the couple moved from their quiet location in Glaisdale to Hutton Rudby, a few miles south of Middlesbrough. With a thriving community of about 1500 residents, there was more activity for Marion than in Glaisdale, and although their new property had a smaller plot, Allan still had somewhere to nurture his love of gardening.

Everything at Hutton Rudby was perfect, and for an active couple in their sixties life could not have been better. They were close to open countryside for frequent rambles, village life was interesting and engaging, and their home town of Middlesbrough was only a short drive away.

9 Langbaurgh Road, Hutton Rudby (present day)

At the turn of the millennium, Allan was a couple of years off his 80th birthday and Marian was in her early 70s. Life was being lived to the full, and although physical activities were not quite what they were, there was plenty going on around the house. Beer was being brewed, demijohns of berry wine bubbled gently through air traps, bread and cakes filled the house with appetite-inducing aromas and jars of home-made jam and marmalade were plentiful.

The good life was not to last; Allan became ill with dementure. Hardly noticeable at first, the symptoms gradually but unrelentingly worsened until by 2008 he needed Marion's full time attention. By then in her 80th year, she was not particularly surprised that she was becoming tired and her energy levels were not what they used to be. She soon realised that there was more to how she felt than the strain of caring for Allan, but she kept her symptoms to herself and tried to carry on as normal. There was a holiday visit from daughter Helen and her family coming up, and grand-daughter Jenny was soon to be married.

Keeping her illness secret from her children, Marion enlisted the help of her niece Wendy. This allowed her to carry on a few more months, but just before Helen's planned visit she took a turn for the worse and was admitted to James Cook Hospital in Middlesbrough where doctors diagnosed t-cell lymphoma. Chemotherapy was not an option because of her advanced years, but blood transfusions and medication postponed the inevitable outcome for a month or two. Marion died in hospital on 12th September 2009, the day before her grand-daughter's wedding.

Allan's dementure meant that he needed constant management, and for a few months he was able to remain at home with the help of door alarms, carers, and overnight supervision. Despite the safety precautions put in place, Allan was found one wintry night two miles from home wandering around a haulage lorry park in the snow.

There was no choice but to admit Allan to a care home, and he moved in to a specialist dementure unit near Richmond, close to where daughter Barbara lived, on 1st February 2010. He was very popular, and lived a contented life there for almost six years. On 20th January 2016

Allan was enjoying his tea when he suffered a ruptured abdominal aortic aneurism and died.

Allan and Marion were cremated at Middlesbrough Crematorium on Acklam Road, less than a mile from where each was born; Marion on 17th September 2009 and Allan on 1st February 2016. Their ashes were scattered in the same place, although six years apart, next to Captain Cook's Monument high up on Easby Moor. It was a location they both loved, and they shared years of happy memories walking in the area.

Close to where the family stayed on holiday in Glaisdale

The memorial stone reads:

THE ASHES OF JAMES W. GOTT AND FLORENCE HIS WIFE ARE SCATTERED IN THE VICINITY OF THIS STONE 1947

Hilda's ashes are scattered next to those of her parents.

www.ingramcontent.com/pod-product-compliance
Lightning Source LLC
Chambersburg PA
CBHW071721090426
42738CB00009B/1836